Peace Journalism in East Africa

This concise edited collection explores the practice of peace journalism in East Africa, focusing specifically on the unique political and economic contexts of Uganda and Kenya.

The book offers a refreshing path toward transformative journalism in East Africa through imbibing pan-African institutional methodological approaches and the African philosophies of *Utu* (humanity), *Umoja* (unity), and *Harambee* (collective responsibility) as news values. Contributions from key academics demonstrate how media practices that are supportive of peace can prevent the escalation of conflict and promote its nonviolent resolution. The chapters cumulatively represent a rich repertoire of experiences and cases that skillfully tell the story of the connections between media and peacebuilding in East Africa, while also avoiding romanticizing peace journalism as an end to itself or using it as an excuse for censorship.

This cutting-edge research book is a valuable resource for academics in journalism, media studies, communication, peace and conflict studies, and sociology.

Fredrick Ogenga is Associate Professor of Communication and Media Studies; Founding Director, Center for Media, Democracy, Peace, and Security, Rongo University; and President of the Peacemaker Corps Foundation Kenya. Ogenga is championing a pan-African journalistic institutional approach for conflict prevention and peacebuilding.

Peace Journalism in East Africa
A Manual for Media Practitioners

Edited by Fredrick Ogenga

Routledge
Taylor & Francis Group

LONDON AND NEW YORK

First published 2020 by Routledge

2 Park Square, Milton Park, Abingdon, Oxon OX14 4RN

605 Third Avenue, New York, NY 10017

Routledge is an imprint of the Taylor & Francis Group, an informa business

First issued in paperback 2022

Publisher's Note

The publisher has gone to great lengths to ensure the quality of this reprint but points out that some imperfections in the original copies may be apparent.

British Library Cataloguing-in-Publication Data
A catalogue record for this book is available from the British Library

Library of Congress Cataloging-in-Publication Data
A catalog record for this book has been requested

ISBN: 978-0-367-25068-3 (hbk)
ISBN: 978-1-03-233827-9 (pbk)
DOI: 10.4324/9780429285844

Typeset in Sabon
by Apex CoVantage, LLC

Contents

Contributors

Victor Bwire is the deputy chief executive officer for Media Council of Kenya.

Gloria Laker is the director of the Peace Journalism Foundation of East Africa in Uganda, prior to which she reported on the Lord's Resistance Army insurgency in northern Uganda.

Jacinta Mwende Maweu is a senior lecturer in the Department of Philosophy and an adjunct lecturer in the School of Journalism and Media Studies at the University of Nairobi.

Fredrick Ogenga is an associate professor of Communication and Media Studies; the founding director of the Center for Media, Democracy, Peace, and Security, Rongo University; and the president of the Peacemaker Corps Foundation, Kenya.

John Oluoch is a senior lecturer in the Department of Communication, Journalism, and Media Studies at Rongo University.

Steven Youngblood is an associate professor and the director of the Center for Global Peace Journalism at Park University, USA. He is also the editor-in-chief of *Peace Journalist* magazine.

Introduction

Fredrick Ogenga

This publication is the outcome of the "East Africa Regional Peace Journalism Training Workshop" for journalists covering conflict and peacebuilding in East Africa. Organized by Rongo University's Center for Media, Democracy, Peace, and Security (CMDPS) in partnership with the African Peacebuilding Network (APN) of the Social Science Research Council (SSRC), the two-day event brought together journalists from five East African countries – Kenya, Rwanda, South Sudan, Tanzania, and Uganda – to develop their capacity for reporting on conflict-related issues in an objective manner based on the tenets of the theory and practice of peace journalism.

The workshop also served as a forum for facilitating discussions and networking between journalists and scholars from diverse East African countries working on peace and conflict at local, national, and regional levels. Participants also learned more about the APN-SSRC, including the opportunities it provides to support research and networking activities between scholars and practitioners across Africa. They also learned about how to effectively use peace-promoting approaches, tools, and platforms for covering and reporting stories on conflict and peacebuilding.

This book brings together and captures the presentations, discussions, and outcomes of the workshop. The chapters that follow are based on the presentations by the lead speakers at the workshop. They explore the various dimensions of violent conflict, particularly the way it is reported in the media and how such reports affect society. This analysis comes against the background of the role some media reports have played in the outbreak of violence across East Africa, particularly in fanning the embers of election-related violence or mass anxiety and fear following terrorist attacks. For example, media coverage of Kenya's disputed 2007 elections contributed to the escalation of the conflict resulting in loss of lives, displacement, and destruction of property. Apart from the adverse impact on the image of Kenya as a peaceful and prosperous nation, reports of communal and political conflict or the threat of violence in other East African states have undermined local, national, and regional efforts at peacebuilding. It is against this background that some media scholars and practitioners underscore the importance of paying more attention to the need for "peace journalism" as a strategy for peacemaking and peacebuilding.

These experts are of the view that sensitivity to peace and the nonviolent prevention and resolution of conflict are best captured within the conceptual framework of "peace journalism" that, in addition to its emphasis on accurate reporting on matters of public interest, employs a variety of techniques to de-escalate social tensions. Peace journalism is not reporting that is wholly or even primarily oriented toward peace at all costs; it does not sacrifice truth and justice for a "law and order" type of peace as defined by the state. Peace journalism brings together certain elements that are essential to promoting peace in East African countries. The enabling elements of this form of journalism include sensitivity, agility, caution, factual information, and self-reflectivity in relation to what media practitioners put into the content of news reports and editorials.

Due to the reality that East African countries vary with respect to the nature of conflicts and the degree of media freedom, these elements may not be practically applicable across the board but will depend on the relevant circumstances. For instance, covering a civil war will differ from reporting on terrorism or political or election-related conflict. However, these elements and the values embedded in peace journalism will help foster a culture of peace and nonviolent conflict resolution across the region. It will also facilitate the creation of a media space within which practitioners, scholars, and other stakeholders can learn from and support one another. This approach to information and knowledge dissemination will foster new insights and help develop innovative journalism.

This publication provides insights and knowledge aimed at strengthening the capacity of media practitioners for improved and ethically sound coverage of conflict and peacebuilding in East Africa, with the goal of improving the prospects for peace and development. It is expected that it will become a manual for those seeking to understand and imbibe the values of peace journalism and reflect them in their day-to-day activities and conflict reporting in ways that bring the fourth estate – journalism – into the mainstream of peacebuilding in East Africa.

In the first chapter, "The Peace Journalism Approach," Steven Youngblood provides an overview and operational definition of peace journalism, outlining its evolution, principles, and giving examples of peace journalism in print media. Making the case for peace journalism, the chapter urges media practitioners to avoid the use of inflammatory language when covering elections and conflicts. To better prepare journalists for peace-centered reporting during conflict situations, the author encourages them to hold in-house peace and election reporting training for reporters covering upcoming elections in Africa. The chapter explores the importance of word choice and news framing as important aspects in the promotion of peace journalism in Africa.

The second chapter, "Peace Journalism in the LRA Conflict" by Gloria Laker, explores the role of peace journalism in ending the Lord's Resistance Army (LRA) insurgency (1988–2006) in northern Uganda, drawing on Laker's own experience as a war reporter. She provides a compelling case study about how a radio station founded by the Ugandan military called "Radio Freedom" morphed into the much larger and more impactful Mega FM radio station, helping to end the LRA conflict by directly reaching out to enemy combatants and persuading them to surrender with an assurance of amnesty. The chapter shows in practical terms how a radio station used its broadcasts to help sow the seeds of peace in northern Uganda, for which it has been widely credited.

The point of departure is the third and fourth chapters by Fredrick Ogenga. In Chapter 3, "Thinking about Community Radio and Beyond for Conflict Management in The North Rift: A Concept Paper," Ogenga problematizes the emerging conflict trend in counties in the North Rift, Kenya, fueled by many issues among them natural resource pressure due to climate change and destruction of the Mau water tower. He points out the urgent need to address these emerging conflict trends in a creative manner that allows grassroots community participation and ownership and, at the same time, utilizing traditional and new media technology arguing that the media has the advantage of wide reach and technical capacity to change attitudes and perceptions for peace and security especially when it considers local contexts and nuances which calls for African ways of seeing for peacebuilding (African Peace Journalism).

Chapter 4 is titled "Hybrid Peace Journalism: Institutional Philosophical Approaches to Peace and Security in Africa." Chapter 3 therefore gives a conceptual overview of a Hybrid (African) Peace Journalism (HPJ) in the context of emerging terrorist threats in Kenya. He explains how his unique approach to peace journalism eclectically combines elements from Western peace journalism and African *gnosis* (lenses) in conflict-sensitive reporting. HPJ is based on development journalism that portrays Africa in a positive light. Hinged upon *Utu* (humanity), *Umoja* (unity), and *Harambee* (collective responsibility) as core African values, this approach also offers a counternarrative to Western-style journalism that tends to focus on sensationalized and largely negative versions of Africa-related news. The chapter also includes information on the several HPJ-related programs at Rongo University, including a master's degree in media, democracy, peace, and security; the Salah Farah Visiting Post-Doctoral Research Fellowship on Media and Terrorism; and the Campus Peace Ambassadors club run by undergraduates studying journalism.

Chapter 5, "Re-Situating Vernacular Media: A Tool for Peace Building among the Abakuria in Kenya" by John Oluoch, examines the place of indigenous languages in media outlets located in rural areas. Focusing on the Abakuria community, the chapter calls for deeper analyses of the suitability of local languages for broadcasts aimed at resolving inter-ethnic conflicts in rural settings. The author is critical of the use of local languages on media platforms for resolving ethnic conflict. It concludes that even though community-based radio stations broadcasting in such languages appear to be the most reliable sources of news and information among the Abakuria, like in many other parts of Kenya, their potential as tools for intra-ethnic conflict mitigation and that of fueling violence cannot be taken for granted.

Victor Bwire's chapter, "Media and Peace in Kenya: Do Journalists Need Different Skills?" interrogates the crisis of credibility facing the Kenyan media. Arguing that the media has lost public trust due to its partisanship, bias, and poor ethical practices, Bwire claims that public trust can be regained if journalists are given better training so that they adhere to objectivity, ethics, and high professional standards in their reporting and gain a greater awareness of their role and influence in society. Like other chapters in this book, he calls for conflict-sensitive in-house training on how to cover controversial or highly contested issues without using language or content that is likely to incite the other side or vice versa.

In Chapter 7, "Peace Journalism and Human Rights," Jacinta Mwende Maweu argues that the media's subordination to the interests of political and economic elites prevents it from practicing a "peace and human rights approach" to journalism. These elites, who more often double up as media owners, are the main perpetrators of human rights violations and undermine media freedom to avoid scrutiny and accountability at the expense of more vulnerable citizens. She claims that the media's power is in its ability to set the news agenda and frame issues objectively. Such a role enables it to promote human rights by keeping the public informed and engaged. This, however, requires a credible and independent press committed to the truth. Taken as a whole, the chapter authors of *East Africa Peace Journalism* offer a compelling case for peace journalism and a practical guide on how peace journalism may best be implemented in an East African setting.

1 The peace journalism approach

Steven Youngblood

Any discussion of peace journalism must begin with a conceptual examination of the term's constitutive parts. Although peace has often been defined simply as the absence of conflict or violence, Norwegian scholar Dr. Johan Galtung, one of the fathers of peace studies (and peace journalism), has written extensively about "positive" and "negative" peace. In this regard, Galtung defines negative peace as the absence of conflict, whereas positive peace consists of conditions where justice, equity, harmony, and so on can flourish.[1]

For the purposes of peace journalism, Galtung's notion of positive peace is particularly useful since peace journalists strive to highlight individuals and initiatives that contribute toward harmonious conditions and to lead constructive public dialogues about issues that pertain to justice and equity.

The American Press Institute defines journalism as "the activity of gathering, assessing, creating, and presenting news and information."[2] According to the *Oxford Dictionary*, it is "the activity or profession of writing for newspapers, magazines, or news websites or preparing news to be broadcast." However, this traditional definition has become problematic in the digital age. Do bloggers practice journalism? Are tweets, Facebook posts, and photos shared on Instagram aspects of journalism in the digital age? Who then is a peace journalist?

A peace journalist is a communicator who considers the consequences of his or her reporting when making reportorial and editorial decisions. In peace journalism, one would be less concerned with the nuances of who is technically a journalist and more worried about the content and impact of the reports/messages disseminated by anyone, be they professional journalists, citizen-journalists, or social media commentators.

Defining peace journalism

In their groundbreaking book, *Peace Journalism*, Jake Lynch and Annabel McGoldrick observe that peace journalism occurs "when editors and reporters make choices – about what to report, and how to report it – that create opportunities for society at large to consider and to value non-violent responses to conflict." Peace journalism

> uses the insights of conflict analysis and transformation to update the concepts of balance, fairness, and accuracy in reporting. It also provides a new road map tracing the connections between journalists, their sources, the stories they cover, and the consequences of their journalism, and builds an awareness of nonviolence and creativity into the practical job of everyday editing and reporting.[3]

The Center for Global Peace Journalism (CGPJ) at Park University (USA) adapts and expands on Lynch and McGoldrick's definition. The CGPJ notes that peace journalism is a practice in which

> editors and reporters make choices that improve the prospects for peace. These choices, including how to frame stories and carefully choosing which words are used, create an atmosphere conducive to peace and supportive of peace initiatives and peacemakers, without compromising the basic principles of good journalism. Peace journalism gives peacemakers a voice while making peace initiatives and non-violent solutions more visible and viable.[4]

Equally important is a consideration of what peace journalism is not. It is not, according to the CGPJ and Lynch, open advocacy for peace. Instead, in Lynch's words, peace journalism is to "give peace a chance."[5]

The origins of peace journalism

As mentioned earlier, peace journalism is a concept developed by Johan Galtung in the early 1960s. In a recent interview, Dr. Galtung said he coined the term because he believed "journalists have to learn to write about peace and core structural issues and to focus on common people." He noted he was encouraged to develop the concept, in part, due to a 1960s' study that showed that foreign news was largely negative; often featuring an actor (bad guy), elite people, and centered on elite countries (Interview, Rongo University, November 20, 2015).

Dr. Galtung's original concept was further developed at the Taplow Court estate in southern England in August 1997 when the estate, which serves as the UK headquarters of Soka Gakkai International, an international Buddhist organization, hosted a meeting with Dr. Galtung, Jake Lynch, and other journalists. At the meeting, participants discussed a plan for merging journalism and peace and conflict studies to work synchronously.[6]

Lynch, spurred by the Taplow meeting, went on to direct a project and website called *Reporting the World*. It was described as "a practical checklist for the ethical reporting of conflicts in the 21st century produced by journalists for journalists." The project, which ran from 2001 to 2005, facilitated a discussion among London journalists about conflict reporting and journalists' role in mitigating, alleviating, and transforming conflicts. *Reporting the World* provided a foundation for the 17 points articulated by Lynch and McGoldrick in *Peace Journalism* in 2005. This first book on peace journalism inspired a number of related titles, including *Peace Journalism, War and Conflict Resolution* by Richard Lance Keeble, John Tulloch, and Florian Zollman in 2010; *Conflict Sensitive Reporting: State of the Art* by Howard Ross in 2009; and Steve Sharp's *Journalism and Conflict in Indonesia: From Reporting Violence to Promoting Peace* in 2013. Other contributions to the literature include *Peace Journalism: The State of the Art* by Dov Shinarand and Wilhelm Kempf in 2007; Wilhelm Kempf's *Readings in Peace Journalism: Foundations, Studies, Perspectives* in 2010; and Steven Youngblood's *Professor Komagum: Teaching Peace Journalism and Battling Insanity in Uganda* in 2012.[7]

A semiannual magazine, *The Peace Journalist*, was launched in 2012 by Park University's CGPJ. *Peace Journalism Insights* is a blog run by the director of CGPJ. Dr. Galtung also writes a weekly editorial for the online outlet known as *Transcend*.[8]

Key principles of peace journalism

Lynch and McGoldrick lay out a number of principles, including a widely distributed chart comparing peace journalism to "war/violence journalism" and a seventeen-point checklist of "what a peace journalist would try to do." In the chart, war/violence journalism is reporting characterized by the spreading of propaganda and "us" versus "them" narratives that demonize "them." It is dominated by reporting that is victory-oriented, reactive, and elite-oriented, and focuses only on the visible effects of violence. Peace journalism is the opposite. It is reporting that is proactive, humanizes the other side, gives voice to everyday people, and discusses solutions.[9]

Four items on Lynch and McGoldrick's 17-point plan for peace journalism focus on the importance of language and particularly the need to avoid language that victimizes ("devastated," "destitute," "defenseless"), is imprecise and emotive ("tragedy," "massacre," "systematic"), demonizes ("vicious," "cruel," "barbaric"), and imprecisely labels ("terrorist," "extremist," "fanatic," "fundamentalist"). Other key points include avoiding reporting about conflict as if it is a zero-sum game (one winner, one loser), reporting about common ground shared by parties involved in the conflict, avoiding reporting only the violent acts and "the horror" and not reporting claims as though they are facts.

However, during the more than ten years since *Peace Journalism*, theorists and practitioners (including the CGPJ) have expanded this original war reporting orientation into other fields of journalistic endeavor, discovering along the way the utility of peace journalism principles to inform and improve practices in reporting politics and elections, terrorism, crime, and human rights. In fact, the peace journalism approach can be used to guide reporting about any type of conflict (political, ethnic, resource disputes, civil unrest, religious) and not just those involving violence.

Keeping in mind peace journalism's applicability to many domains, the CGPJ has devised a ten-point list that describes the elements of peace journalism.

Peace journalism elements

- PJ [peace journalism] is proactive; it examines the causes of conflict and leads discussions about solutions.
- PJ looks to unite parties rather than divide them and eschews oversimplified "us versus them" and "good guy versus bad guy" reporting.
- Peace reporters reject official propaganda and instead seek facts from all sources.
- PJ is balanced, covering issues/suffering/peace proposals from all sides of a conflict.
- PJ gives voice to the voiceless, instead of just reporting for and about elites and those in power.

- Peace journalists provide depth and context rather than just superficial and sensational "blow by blow" accounts of violence and conflict.
- Peace journalists consider the consequences of their reporting.
- Peace journalists carefully choose and analyze the words they use; they that carelessly selected words are often inflammatory.
- Peace journalists thoughtfully select the images they use understanding that they can misrepresent an event, exacerbate an already dire situation, and re-victimize those who have suffered.
- Peace Journalists offer counter-narratives that debunk media created or otherwise perpetuated stereotypes, myths, and misperceptions

Source: CGPJ.

These ten peace journalism principles and those laid out by Lynch and McGoldrick were created in response to sensational and irresponsible reporting that ignored or devalued peaceful responses to conflict while exacerbating already tense, contentious, and difficult situations.

Example of peace journalism

Let us begin with a comparison between "traditional" journalism and peace journalism. An example of a news story framed according to traditional reporting is as follows:

> *Gatu City, Republic of Gatu* – Green Party Presidential Candidate Moses Akena said yesterday that Blue Party nominee Steven Oguti has been stealing money from the state treasury for many years, and that's why Oguti has been able to afford nice cars and fancy vacations.
> "This kind of thievery is typical of people from his tribe," Akena observed. "It is clear that Oguti and those like him are no-good snakes."
> Further, Akena said that Oguti's corruption will extend to the upcoming election. "We know if he wins, that he will be cheating. Now the question is, what will we do about this? Will we stand by and let him steal from us?"
> Akena went on to compare his manifesto to that of his opponent. Akena said the Green Party promises to tarmac (pave) 1,000 km

of roads per year if elected. He also said that they will hire 2,000 more primary school teachers when they come to power.

Source: CGPJ

This traditional style of reporting is unbalanced and one-sided with the accused given no opportunity to respond. It depends on only one source and reports his words as the truth. It is clear that the reporter is being used to spread political propaganda and rumors. The story widens divisions within this society and could even possibly incite violence ("will we let him steal from us?"). Also, Akena is not held accountable for his statements. How will he pay for the new roads and teachers? How much will these things cost?

In contrast, the following is the same story, this time framed using a peace journalism approach:

> *Gatu City, Republic of Gatu* – Two of Gatu's presidential candidates continue to engage in a campaign of mudslinging while two other candidates yesterday pledged to stick to issues.
>
> At a press conference yesterday, Green Party Presidential Candidate Moses Akena made unsubstantiated charges against one of his opponents, Blue Party nominee Steven Oguti. Akena did briefly discuss his platform, including promises to tarmac 1,000 km of roads and hire 2,000 more primary teachers, but did not explain how or if these projects could be financially realized. Meanwhile, Oguti responded with similar personal attacks against Akena. When pressed about roads and schools, he promised to issue a manifesto on these issues tomorrow.
>
> Several voters interviewed are tired of the mudslinging. Gatu City resident Stephanie Mulumba said, "I wish they'd talk about things that really matter. How can I afford to send my son to school? That's what I really care about."
>
> As Oguti finished meeting the press, Purple Party candidate Alex Busiga and Orange Party candidate Betty Aciro held their own joint press conference where they pledged to discuss issues in this election. "The people want to know about roads and hospitals, and that's what I'm going to talk about," Aciro said. However, neither candidate was ready to discuss their positions on these issues in detail.
>
> *Source:* CGPJ

This version of the story is better because it is balanced among many parties and uses multiple sources. In this version, personal attacks are not aired, only referenced (and discredited). There is neither ethnic name-calling nor potentially provocative content. Claims are not presented as facts. More prominent play is given to real issues that affect average people, who are quoted in the story. Also, political promises are exposed – what are their cost and feasibility?

Framing and word choice

Two key elements of peace journalism involve framing and word choice. The simplest definition of framing in journalism is the way journalists organize and present news. This includes which aspects of stories to emphasize, what to minimize, and what to ignore. According to framing theory, the media serves as a mediator between individuals and society and between the audience and the world around them. Sociologist and media scholar Gaye Tuchman argued that

> the meaning of the events is given by the journalist through the news, because taken itself an event has no significance. It is the imposition of a frame of other ordered events that allows recognition of facts and the attribution of significance.[10]

It is important for peace journalists to recognize the power of the media to create meaning and, thus, structure societal discourses. Unfortunately, this power has often been used by some journalists to create narratives that are superficial, that are lacking in context, and that tend to reinforce stereotypes. Peace journalism, conversely, seeks to offer counternarratives and to frame stories in such a way as to encourage a more nuanced, thorough, and constructive societal conversation.

The importance of responsible framing is matched only by the importance of word choice. As Lynch and McGoldrick have stated, peace journalists must take care not to use words that are demonizing, victimizing, and inflammatory.[11] They understand that carelessly selected words can be anger-inducing, misleading, or divisive.

There are many words that journalists regularly and carelessly use that add only emotion and no substance to a story. For example, how many people have to die for an event to become a "massacre"? Or how about the adjectives "brutal," "callous," "slaughter," "grim," "monstrous"? What exactly constitutes a tragedy? And who is a martyr? The fact is that all of these words and their synonyms are subjective and imprecise. If a journalist (or peace journalist) is to adhere to the principle of objectivity and impartiality, and if these emotive words are inherently subjective, this alone should be sufficient reason to omit such language. Peace journalism teaches that if one hundred people were killed, we simply write that 100 people were killed. Peace journalists write the facts and let the reader or listener make their own subjective decisions as to whether the event is a tragedy or a massacre.

Peace and conflict theory and peace journalism

Peace journalists need also be aware of their responsibility in mitigating two seldom-considered nonphysical types of violence distinguished by Galtung: structural and cultural. "Structural violence" refers to institutionalized societal conditions that may harm citizens and prevent them from meeting their basic needs. These conditions include social oppression, discrimination, marginalization, sexism, racism, and economic injustice.[12] Specifically, Galtung first defines violence as "avoidable impairment of fundamental human needs or, to put it in more general terms, the impairment of human life, which lowers the actual degree to which someone is able to meet their needs below that which would otherwise be possible." The first aspect of this definition to note is the inclusion of the word *avoidable*.[13]

By "cultural violence," Galtung means "those aspects of culture, the symbolic sphere of our existence, exemplified by religion and ideology, language and art, empirical science and formal science (logic, mathematics) that can be used to justify or legitimize direct or structural violence." Put another way, "cultural violence is any aspect (often symbolic) of a culture that can be used to legitimize violence."[14] Rather than thinking of cultural and structural violence as separate entities, a peace journalist would consider them two branches of the same tree since they are both "indirect and insidious." Both are "built into the very nature of social, cultural, and economic institutions. For example, both ancient Egypt and imperial Rome were highly despotic, although they were technically in states of negative peace for long periods of time." The connections between these theories and the practice of peace journalism are clear. Peace journalists, and indeed all responsible journalists, must discuss and expose conditions like sexism, racism, and economic discrimination that compose structural violence instead of merely reporting on the direct violence (like riots) that results from these conditions. Structural violence reporting requires the kind of nuance and context that is a bedrock principle of peace reporting – reporting that seeks, after all, to enable Galtung's notion of "positive peace."

Thus, peace journalists should lead community dialogues about the elements of and solutions for mitigating cultural violence. Again, traditional journalism might typically report about these issues only when they foment direct violence (e.g., Christian attacks on Muslims) or sensational confrontation (e.g., creationists vs. biologists at a school board meeting). By reporting contextually, peace journalists can move beyond these superficial narratives by analyzing how religion, science, language, and art are used to explain or legitimize direct or structural violence.

Notes

1 Johan Galtung, *Peace by Peaceful Means: Peace and Conflict, Development and Civilization* (London: SAGE Publications, 1996).
2 American Press Institute, "What Is Journalism," www.americanpressinstitute. org/journalism-essentials/what-is-journalism/
3 Jake Lynch and Annabel McGoldrick, *Peace Journalism* (Stroud, UK: Hawthorn Press, 2005), 5.
4 "Peace Journalism: An Introduction," *Park University Center for Global Peace Journalism*, www.park.edu/academics/explore-majors-programs/ peace-journalism-minor/center-global-peace-journalism-2/
5 Jake Lynch, "What Is Peace Journalism," *TRANSCEND Media Service*, www. transcend.org/tms/about-peace-journalism/1-what-is-peace-journalism/
6 Jake Lynch, "Peace Journalism for Journalists," *TRANSCEND Media Service*, www.transcend.org/tms/about-peace-journalism/2-peace-journalism- for-journalists/
7 Richard Lance Keeble, "John Tulloch, and Florian Zollman," in *Peace Journalism, War and Conflict Resolution* (New York: Peter Lang, 2010); Howard Ross, *Conflict Sensitive Reporting: State of the Art* (Paris: UNESCO, 2009); Steve Sharp, *Journalism and Conflict in Indonesia: From Reporting Violence to Promoting Peace* (New York: Routledge 2013); Dov Shinar and Wilhelm Kempf, eds., *Peace Journalism: The State of the Art* (Berlin: Regener, 2007); Wilhelm Kempf, "Conflict Prevention and the Media," in *Readings in Peace Journalism: Foundations, Studies, Perspectives*, ed. Wilhelm Kempf (Berlin: Regener, 2010), 27–37; Steven Youngblood, *Professor Komagum: Teaching Peace Journalism and Battling Insanity in Uganda* (New York: Unlimited Publishing, 2012).
8 See Steven Youngblood's blog, http://stevenyoungblood.blogspot.com; Johan Galtung blogs here, www.transcend.org/tms/
9 Lynch and McGoldrick, *Peace Journalism*, 6.
10 Gaye Tuchman, *Making News: A Study in the Construction of Reality* (New York: The Free Press, 1978), 4.
11 Lynch and McGoldrick, *Peace Journalism*, 6.
12 David Barash and Charles Webel, *Peace and Conflict Studies*, 3rd ed. (Thousand Oaks: Sage Publications, 2014).
13 Kathleen Ho, "Structural Violence as a Human Rights Violation," *Essex Human RightsReview* 4, no. 2 (2007): 3–4.
14 Johan Galtung, "Cultural Violence," *Journal of Peace Research* 27, no. 3 (1990): 291–305.

2 Peace journalism in the LRA conflict

Gloria Laker

The LRA conflict

The Lord's Resistance Army (LRA) insurgency began in 1988 with the goal of overthrowing President Yoweri Museveni's government. Its origins can be traced to the Holy Spirit Movement (HSM), a cult-like rebel group led by the late Alice Auma Lakwena, who claimed the Holy Spirit had ordered her to overthrow President Museveni's government due to its alleged unfair treatment of the Acholi, a Luo Nilotic tribe in northern Uganda. The HSM was defeated near Jinja in eastern Uganda and fled to Ifo refugee camp near Dadaab in Kenya, where she lived for more than ten years and later died.[1] In 1988, Shortly after Lakwena's defeat, Joseph Kony, believed to be her cousin, turned the remnants of HSM into the LRA. Kony and his LRA planned to rule Uganda based on the Ten Commandments, which was quickly rejected. When they lost support, he turned his anger on innocent civilians, especially his own Acholi ethnic group. In frustration, Kony began abducting children as a form of recruitment to enlarge his ranks and gain publicity across the world. Together with his commanders, he looted, raped, raided homes, and planted landmines.[2] The LRA also went as far as maiming civilians – cutting off ears, noses, and lips – as a punishment for reporting on LRA activities to government soldiers.

As the war intensified, Kony's reliance on child soldiers drastically increased. According to estimates, more than 80 percent of Kony's fighters were believed to be children.[3] These underaged fighters were often given ranks to boost their morale to carry out more killings, abductions, and destruction. They were also promised top positions in government if the LRA took over power from Museveni. Such promises emboldened the child soldiers and turned them into cold-blooded killers who participated directly in most of these atrocities committed during the war that resulted in the deaths of more than 100,000 people.

This was the conflict I had to report about. My colleagues and I did our best to inform the world about the atrocities committed in northern Uganda. At the time, it was difficult to provide a balanced report because we had no access to the rebels, which meant that we frequently gave one-sided reports. The few LRA collaborators we knew gave us contradictory and diversionary information, so we could not trust them. There was also some bias in the coverage of the conflict, with varying levels of exaggeration and misreporting. Some newspapers took advantage of the situation and would run very alarming headlines with the intention of increasing their sales, which had the effect of further traumatizing the beleaguered local population. For example, it was reported ahead of planned negotiations in the early days of the peace efforts that some elders had received money from the government side. It is believed that this particular report resulted in LRA rebels killing the elders, which disrupted peace efforts. In another case, reports of rotten relief food being supplied to internally displaced persons (IDPs) camps had a negative impact on food distribution. Rather than reporting that only two bags of maize flour were found to be rotten, media reports gave the alarming impression that all the relief food being sent to IDPs was unfit for human consumption, forcing authorities to stop food distribution for a time, which adversely affected the IDPs.

Frequent media reports of President Museveni's ultimatums to LRA rebels had a negative impact on the peace process and may have contributed to the committing of more atrocities. Each time the media reported that the president had given the rebels an ultimatum of two weeks to either sign a peace agreement or else he would finish them, the rebels would raid even more villages. If the media had avoided sensationalism and reported such statements according to the tenets of peace journalism, it would have likely had a less negative impact.

The evolution of peace journalism in northern Uganda

Despite the numerous challenges faced by the media, we collectively reported on the conflict. Doing so became easier through networking and the initiation of a collaboration mechanism among reporters. This enabled journalists to share tips, which increased coverage of the war and as a result turned international attention toward the LRA conflict.

After years of failed military interventions and a series of futile peace talks, the Ugandan army opted to invest in "peace media" in addition to military operations and, in 1998, established the first peace radio station in Gulu town called Radio Freedom. This medium was used to communicate to displaced persons and rebels, allowing the government to give child soldiers an assurance of safety should they escape from and denounce the rebel LRA group. As a result, a number of fighters slowly began escaping from the LRA camps – a positive step in the search for peace.

Successful peace journalism strategies in ending the LRA conflict

On realizing the contribution made by Radio Freedom, the first community peace radio in Uganda, donors then started looking to well-trained media practitioners and radio programming as a way to promote peace during the civil war and later in the postconflict period. Between 1999 and 2002, Britain's Department for International Development (DFID) strongly supported the use of radio programs to persuade rebels to abandon fighting the government. DFID funded the establishment of Mega FM radio station in Gulu, which the government merged with Radio Freedom to become one of the major radio stations that broadcasted peace media programs in northern Uganda. With improved signal strength, Mega FM went on the air in August 2002 covering parts of southern Sudan, eastern Democratic Republic of Congo, and the wider northern Uganda region. The station broadcasted information about conflict and development and was geared toward conflict resolution by promoting the peace process. Ogena Lacambel, the host of Mega FM's flagship Luo-language program, *Dwog Pacho* (*Come Back Home*), would invite former child soldiers to share their stories on the radio.

Today, Mega FM still has several peacebuilding programs including *Kabake* (community dialogue) and *Teyat* (stakeholders' dialogue), open dialogue, and live call-in shows. Community members and LRA returnees are often featured in these programs appealing to those still fighting in the bush to return home. Lacambel has continued his *Come Back Home* program to boost anti-LRA efforts in the Central African Republic (CAR), where he travels to interview displaced persons, refugees, and potential returnees for his program, thus making radio an effective medium and tool for peace journalism in the current peace process in northern Uganda.

To reinforce the peace journalism approach, hundreds of local journalists were trained in peace and conflict-sensitive journalism by international media development agencies like Internews, the Center for Global Peace Journalism, Human Rights Focus, Conciliation Resources, the Institute for War and Peace Reporting, and Germany's DW Akademie. Trainees were assessed on the potential impact of their reporting about the peace process. A number of community radio stations dedicated to peace journalism were set up and are still active today.

One unique media training initiative carried out by Internews that hundreds of peace journalists benefited from was themed "From the Juba peace conference to the community." It was aimed at boosting the Juba peace process by allowing peace journalism to play a key role in the peace talks that contributed to a cessation of hostilities agreement in the form of the Comprehensive Peace Agreement between the Sudanese Peoples Liberation Movement and the government of Sudan in 2005.

Peace reporting awards

Peace reporting awards – in the form of equipment, cash, or scholarships – for excellence in conflict coverage have been created. This has motivated many reporters to report on conflicts from peace journalism perspectives.

Media/NGO partnerships

A number of nongovernmental organizations (NGOs) have partnered with peace journalists in the region to produce messages about peaceful reconciliation, many of which still play on some radio stations today. The evidence suggests that the peace journalism approach was useful in mobilizing people and reaching out to rebels. More than 22,000 child soldiers and commanders responded to the appeal to abandon the war, significantly weakening the LRA. Ending the LRA conflict would have been more difficult without the application of various peace journalism tools, including well-researched and balanced news reports, public service announcements, talk shows, focus group discussions, drama and songs, and school debates.

Conclusion

The northern Uganda experience teaches us that well-designed peace journalism programs involving trained reporters can contribute greatly towards ending violent conflict and can potentially help in ending other conflicts in the Great Lakes region. One thing to bear in mind is that an effective peace journalism approach goes beyond merely reporting the news to engage the community by promoting peace initiative.

Notes

1 Eric Westervelt, "Resistance Army Leader in Kenya After 'Holy War'," *NPR*, November 12, 2005, www.npr.org/templates/story/story.php?storyId=5010 520?storyId=5010520

2 Ruddy Doom and Koen Vlassenroot, "Kony's Message: A New Koine? The Lord's Resistance Army in Northern Uganda," *African Affairs* 98, no. 390 (1999): 5–36.

3 Christopher Blattman and Jeannie Anna, "On the Nature and Causes of LRA Abduction: What the Abductees Say," in *The Lord's Resistance Army: Myth and Reality*, eds. Tim Allen and Koen Vlassenroot (London and New York: Zed Books, 2010), 132–155.

3 Thinking about community radio and beyond for conflict management in the North Rift

A concept paper

Fredrick Ogenga

Introduction

In order for us to come up with creative and more sustainable ways of solving conflicts, more so in environments characterized by diminishing natural resources, erratic weather patterns due to climate change, and population pressure that are the defining characteristics of the North Rift region of Kenya, then we must first explore the locally available infrastructures for peacebuilding. This is so because more often than not, the government has pursued foreign interventions dictated from Nairobi that involve political pressure and the use of force through police and the military as well as other sophisticated security measures championed by NGAO (National Government Administrative Officers). Unfortunately, these measures have failed to bring peace in the region owing to the fact that they are being applied in rural settings, with poor access to water, roads, and telecommunication, making it difficult to mobilize the much-needed support and emergency response when conflict emerges – this has been the reality in the North Rift. This is why it is becoming increasingly important to explore the potential of locally available infrastructure for peace and security, one of which is the focus of this chapter, such as (grassroots media like radio/community radio) to help solve conflicts constructively.

Community radio and social media give room for the much-needed dialogue and deliberation in cases of conflict. They can be the tools for community mobilization, mobilization of resources and distress calls given the nature of their content which is deliverable in local dialect or vernacular. However, they are not self-sufficient, and that is why this chapter calls for going beyond community radio to include social media and user-generated content therein in the context of citizen journalism. In addition, there being little research on the links among vernacular radio, social media, and violence means that there is a research gap that needs to be adequately addressed. Studies have focused on the negative role of the media in escalating conflict such as the 2007 postelection violence in Kenya and the Rwandan genocide. In this context, it has been observed that the positive role that the media plays in conflict resolution has been undermined. Therefore, it is critical that we begin examining the positive role of media, such as community radio, in peacebuilding. It is also critical that we do not risk romanticizing the role of community radio as a one-stop shop for all community problems by appraising the combined used of other forms of media technology such as social media.

Community radio and social media put into combined use can be great tools for peacebuilding in Kenya, and just how to tap their role is to actively appraise their potential through participatory initiatives such as those that train media stakeholders (training of trainers), community radio journalists, and social media users in how to responsibly manage user-generated content. There should also be well-crafted media literacy activities targeting citizen journalists (netizens) in cyber-democracy. Social media sensitization for peace and conflict resolution content delivery and practical deliverables that involve the community at large through vernacular to encourage ownership and commitment are very important for setting development agendas at the grassroots level such as peacebuilding.

If this is done well, the positive contribution of media in conflict resolution will be realized. However, due to the complex nature of communities and individuals therein given the complicated geography of the North Rift region, ethnic composition and other factors we argue that there is equally an important measure that we need to undertake as responsible citizens. The latter should understand the individualized nature of security in a perspective that underscores the salience of an individual as part of the national and county security architecture just as much as he or she is an extension of the community and society. Therefore, the individual has a significant role to play in peace and security, especially in the context of modern communication technology found in Web 2.0 or social media platforms.

Social media platforms have provided the necessary local and international infrastructure in peace and conflict discourses and can now either be positively or negatively exploited with varied consequences. Recently, we were made aware of how Facebook was used for political propaganda and electoral manipulation in different parts of the world including Kenyan and the United States. Social networks such as WhatsApp and Twitter are used in various ways in our daily interactive environment and can be positively exploited in everyday life as virtual transnational spaces for peacebuilding.

Given that Kenya's internet cell phone–access level is arguably among the highest globally, it means that there is an increasing percentage of cell phone ownership even among the rural population. Internet-enabled cell phones can be used to enhance the conflict resolution potential of community radio and thus our conceptual argument "beyond community radio," which helps to avoid romanticizing community radio interventions. So this chapter explores the role of journalism in the context of citizen journalism and user-generated content as provided for through social media. This brings to the fore two conflicting issues surrounding the questions of what entails authentic journalism viz-à-viz citizen journalism and, consequently, African journalism. The former implies active journalism through trained community personnel, and the latter, the ability to responsibly manage user-generated content by social media users about virtually anything, including fake news, through media literacy training programs and policy legislation. In the latter, Uganda, for example, instituted a social media tax while in Kenya there are illegalities related to the circulation of certain contents that are deemed unethical.

So how can we take advantage of these conflicting issues to interrogate journalistic practice to come up with an approach that speaks truth to the local context found in Africanized journalism which is journalism with African lenses (African Peace Journalism)? The latter borrows from the Western version of peace journalism that entails conflict sensitive reporting and involves bringing multiple voices in the negotiating table for conflict resolution and peacebuilding. African Peace Journalism consists of African philosophies of *Utu* (humanity), *Umoja* (unity) and *Harambee* (collective responsibility) as key tenets, radically departing from Western sensational journalism led by "if it bleeds it leads" aphorism and "good news in bad news."[1] The approach should be one that considers the relevance of community radio and media literacy on social media platforms usually accessed via cellphone technology. This implies that community radio training of trainers (ToT) targeting active journalists in community radio stations in the North Rift and community social media sensitization through community or citizen participation on how to exploit user-generated content for peacebuilding through social media are approaches that would boost the positive role of media technologies in peacebuilding efforts and offer the best path to peace in the North Rift unlike the currently failing material security interventions by the state.

This chapter argues that conducting a ToT module on community radio for conflict resolution and peacebuilding is crucial, followed by piloting and establishing existing community radio stations in the

Great Rift, through a baseline survey, and using them for peacebuilding and conflict resolution by encouraging local participation. The mapped community radio stations would thus be used as the entry points to spreading conflict resolution, crime and violence prevention training and output-oriented interventions in the North Rift and surrounding counties. The social media aspect made possible through internet-enabled cell phones would therefore be blended in the approach to extend the scope of the methodology beyond community radio for peacebuilding. It is important to note that currently, the potential of these radio stations and social media networks in preventing and solving conflicts and other forms of crime and violence is underexploited. Conclusively, the output of the proposed theoretical and practical methodological approach would be measured through deliverables that can be quantified and qualified as shall be seen later in this chapter.

The power of vernacular radio

The longitude and latitude of vernacular mass media broadcasting landscape in Kenya have changed over the last decade under the management of the Communication Authority of Kenya, which licenses stations that broadcast in vernacular languages. Kameme FM that broadcasts in the Kikuyu language was the first pure vernacular station to be set up in 2000, which eventually led to a proliferation of a number of commercial, state-run, and community-based vernacular stations. Vernacular radio stations, in particular, have exploded with the latest data showing that they have increased tenfold over the last decade from 10 in 1999 to more than 120 in 2015. In total, active FM radio stations in Kenya are more than 100. Some of the stations which are on air today include the controversial Kass FM and Chamgei FM (Kalenjin); Coro, Kameme, and Inooro FM (Gikuyu); Ramogi FM, Radio Lake Victoria, Lolwe FM, and Radio Mayienga (Luo); Mulembe FM and Sulwe FM (Luhya); Musyi FM (Kamba); and Egesa FM (Gusii), among others. The problem is that these stations are commercial stations, and they are the ones caught up in the Western journalistic "good news is bad news" aphorism approach that works to undermine peace and security in Kenya. Interestingly, these commercial radio stations have overshadowed community radio, yet the latter, usually not for profit, carries with it the aspirations, desires, fears, and frustrations of the community in a more vocal manner, local language notwithstanding. What makes community radio special is that they are owned by the community, serve the interests of the community and, above all, like vernacular FM stations, also broadcast in vernacular.

It is on record of how vernacular broadcasting can be instrumental in helping developing countries such as Kenya and rural communities combat economic, political, educational, health and social-cultural challenges, ranging from ethnic tensions, natural resource conflict, human rights abuses and corruption in government. Low-literacy levels in rural areas and health issues such as infant mortality, maternal deaths, and communicable diseases could be best addressed by tailor-made radio programs that are broadcast in respective vernacular languages. In addition, radio is affordable and currently with media convergence; it can be freely accessed through cell phones. Considering that cell phone penetration in rural Kenya is relatively high, then it implies that vernacular radio that speaks to the local context can really work wonders in conflict resolution due to the high audience reach and communal feeling of ownership and commitment that is natured through grassroots participation:[2]

> The media, whether traditional (e.g. radio, television and newspapers) or contemporary (21st century) media (e.g. internet and mobile telephony) can be a potent tool either for fomenting and escalating conflict or for ameliorating and resolving it. This notion is fortified with the example of the Rwandan genocide of 1994 where a private radio establishment, *Radio Television Libre des Mille Collines*, was used to rally one ethnic group to commit massacres and try to wipe out another group. The use of the mass media to mitigate inter-ethnic tempers during the Kenyan postelection violence in late 2007 and early 2008 is a well-documented example of media use for conflict de-escalation and resolution.[3]

The media in Kenya, although vibrant, has played a flip-flopping role when it comes to political conflict. In the 2007 general elections, for example, Kenya's vibrant media has been accused of having been ill prepared for the 2007–08 postelection violence that rocked the country as a result of the disputed presidential results.[4] The media failed to set an agenda for peace. It is well known that the media sets agendas and uses values such as prominence (journalists quoting renowned public figures when reporting news stories) to satisfy the interests of the public. However, the public has often been dissatisfied with the media, which has compelled them to devise their own ways of sharing newsworthy information through technology (citizen journalism) leading to the emergence of cyber-citizenship and therein cyber-democracy. However, these forms of virtual realities through internet content sharing can be dangerously exploited to create hatred and animosity and therein conflict. Therefore, it is prudent to have media literacy sensitization programs to avoid propaganda that may lead to conflict in the community.

> Theoretically, web 2.0 sharing could be seen as a kind of revolution [citizen journalism] within the public getting into a trade long held jealously mainly by conventional journalists. What accounts for the fact that a trade, whose mastery requires training on its techniques and specific norms, gets invaded by untutored minds?[5]

The reason why there was violence in 2007 elections in Kenya, for example, is that the mainstream media failed to provide leadership and by default gave the responsibility of reporting what was happening in the ethnically charged election in Kenya to untutored minds on social media through citizen journalism. Prior to the 2007 elections the media did a tremendous job covering campaigns and providing air time and space for candidates to reach the masses. They also did well in releasing opinion polls that proved largely correct in predicting the outcome of parliamentary elections. One reason for the contested presidential election is that the media carried extensive coverage of the voting process and released unofficial results that did not match the official ones. The latter was worsened by the media shut down that followed marking the beginning of direct state influence of media operation following controversial elections.

While the Kenyan media can be praised for staying away of sensationalism in 2007 where they seemed to have understood that the right to peace outweighed the right of Kenyans to know (freedom to receive information) which tribe was killing which and in what manner; information that would only have aggravated the situation[6] the postelection conflict was used by the state to justify media shutdown infringing on the rights of citizens as stipulated in articles 34 and 35 of the Kenyan constitution. This violation was repeated again in the 2017 general elections evidenced through state-sponsored media shutdown justifying the recent wave of increased social media use in politics.

The 2017 elections and the attendant media shutdown were actually turning points for both the Kenyan media regarding its public watchdog role and social media as a new entry in Kenya's political and economic public sphere. During the elections, the media seemed to be confused and boxed into the agenda of the Jubilee (ruling party) ruling class displaying open bias, taking sides and lacking journalistic moral ethics and professionalism by hiding the truth. But it is the concern that the Kenyan media is becoming more of a lap dog that lends urgency to the argument in this chapter for community radio and social media as alternatives to mainstream media and complementary tools for conflict resolution and peacebuilding, albeit after media literacy training.

The 2017 elections were a radical mainstream media "style of reporting" departure from 2013. In the 2013 elections, sections of the Kenyan media played a crucial role in informing, educating and providing space for dialogue and propagation of a spirit of peace, tranquility, and restraint from acts of violence during elections. However, they equally showed a considerably high degree of self-censorship with debatable consequences regarding the peace and security agenda and played a questionable watchdog role. Self-censorship role before, during, and after the 2013 elections made the media very cautious, restrained and careful when attempting to unmask the truth about that election due to the prevailing peace and security discourse in the country at that time which compelled many people to work towards avoiding a repeat of the 2007/08 violence.[7] With this reality in mind, community radio can complement the peace and security architecture by filling in some of the aforementioned peacebuilding gaps created through social media.

Community radio and peacebuilding in Kenya

Community radio can play a very important role in conflict resolution and peacebuilding in a rural environment often with poor transport and communication infrastructure that makes it difficult for stakeholders to respond timely in the event of a conflict. However, the key issue in peacebuilding is conflict prevention, a role that can be well played by radio setup or stationed in the community. When community members participate in discussions about peace in a familiar language, usually vernacular, then they are taking personal initiative and becoming individual agents of security in the broader peace and security architectural framework:

> Community radio are stationed in rural areas and there is an advantage because Kenya's rural population depends on the radio as the most readily available source of important information and news. The information and broadcasting industry has exponentially developed and has a great potential to provide rural population with much benefits that include access to information and educational material available in different languages and forms.[8]

Community radio can be used for mobilization and education on how to share natural resources to avoid conflicts. Most recently, we have witnessed natural resource conflicts in the North Rift related to population pressure, the discovery of oil and other minerals and a lack of grazing pasture due to environmental degradation and climate change. Conflict within homogeneous groups is intimately connected to conflict between heterogeneous groups, which therefore means that for us to have a full understanding of the nature and scale of conflict in the North Rift region and how to mitigate and prevent it, we must completely understand its ethnic dimension without which it would be impossible to have a better grasp of the forces responsible for their generation whether they are inter-ethnic or intra-ethnic and how to respond to intra-ethnic cohesion and fragmentation. The intra-ethnic conflict experienced in the North Rift would thus provide a useful perspective on the nature of group identities, highlighting the mutable characters of group boundaries and the need for response mechanisms that move beyond fixed assumptions of ethnic differences and stereotypes. These are issues that need to be nuanced and contextualized. Some of these response mechanisms are what this chapter conceptualizes.[9]

The chapter therefore argues for the support alternative forms of grassroots media as softer and ideological approaches of resolving or ameliorating long-standing ethnic conflicts in Kenya through some African values of humanity, unity, and collective responsibility. Ethnic harmony is a critical ingredient of nationalism and a critical element that gives direction to development campaigns for education, health, infrastructure, and many more. No society can develop amid incessant violent conflict as witnessed among the communities in the North Rift. This chapter conceptualizes its core argument through recognizing that, first and foremost, the media plays a mutual and reciprocal role in society and helps shape society. The media is therefore a critical peacebuilding infrastructure that should not be taken for granted. Community media, social media conflict resolution, and peacebuilding approaches that use a methodology that recognizes that the relationship between the media and society is mutual and reciprocal wherein the media helps shape the society as the society shapes the media in an interdependence that is inseparable best serves the interests of the community and perhaps have the best chance of success in conflict resolution and peacebuilding in Africa.

Consequently, mass media delivered via vernacular is a significant force to the culture of those who share in that language, particularly in terms of their life and social interactions and collective aspirations as a people. The media has the ability to set agendas and re-create culture through repetition and emphasis regarding certain aspects of the society through mass media messages and these messages promote not only products but also moods, attitudes, beliefs, behavior, and a sense of what is and is not important to them as a people. In the same vein, the message of peace can be broadcast with similar energy for peacebuilding in the North Rift.

Role of media in conflict resolution

A number of organizations like the Center for Media, Democracy, Peace, and Security, Rongo University, have begun considering how to create a situation in a conflict and postconflict environment that allows the media to play a constructive role in tackling conflict, taking account of its true role. It has been increasingly recognized that an effective media is an essential part of preventing violent conflict from breaking out, as well as being an important element in its resolution should it break out due to its sophisticated nature and technical capacity. If this creativity is well captured, natured, and replicated, it may result in a more comprehensive and coherent policy environment for conflict resolution and peacebuilding. The most important aspect of conflict resolution and peacebuilding is the element of participation and ownership. The community media and social media approach suggested here considers the local context and local nuance as crucial determinants of success. When community members directly participate in radio broadcasting through community radio and when other netizens equally generate media content (user-generated content) through social media using their cell phones regarding peace and security issues, then the chances of success are higher. However, whatever content that is being produced should resonate well with local cultures, bringing to sharp focus debates on African journalism and citizen journalism as opposed to Western sensationalism that has resulted in escalating conflicts in Kenya and different parts of the world. In the space of grassroots dialogue, Web 2.0 social media platforms such as Facebook, Twitter, and WhatsApp have an equal potential of playing a crucial role.

Social media: the Twitter *baraza*

Perhaps the most successful experiment on the role of social media and peacebuilding was uncovered through a research done in Rift Valley in Kenya by Duncan Omanga[10] called the Twitter *baraza* (a conflict resolution apparatus chaired by village elders) that shows how social media can be used for conflict resolution and peacebuilding at the village level by those in authority in the NGAO structure such as a village elder and the chief. A chief in Nakuru known as Kariuki established a

Twitter *baraza* where he followed issues happening in the community from those interacting with him. Omanga observed:

> In the first days after setting up his Twitter account Chief Kariuki's tweets reflected his function as a chief and his religious convictions. In addition to sending out invitations for *baraza* meetings, Chief Kariuki used Twitter as an online *baraza* or forum, sharing information in his tweets that would normally be shared at the *baraza*. Chief Kariuki's tweets show that the formal content of *barazas* has not changed much since the 80s despite Chief Kariuki's experiment with a new medium. The tweets serve as an 'online gathering' to establish pro forma consensus rather than allow for debate, passing government directives or policies on health, agriculture or civic issues, on to the public. Chief Kariuki tweets announcing a polio vaccination campaign, free medical clinic, or a crime report, with religious messages in a way that would not be possible in the *baraza*.[11]

The initiative recorded success in preventing conflict and combating crime in Nakuru, and it actually is the kind of social media extension to community radio envisaged in this chapter. It is necessary to complement community media that has been mistaken as the one-stop shop when it comes to conflict resolution and peacebuilding. If, for instance, Twitter and other social media spaces are creatively integrated and utilized, then conflict can be prevented or responded to in a manner that is likely going to save more lives and property and limit the extent of losses. However, it will take more effort and training on media literacy (including community and social media literacy) for the suggested complementary media makeup to be successful, and that is why this chapter calls for capacity-building training interventions at the output level for inventing an African-sensitive journalism.

African media, African journalism

As we seek to conceptualize what would be considered African sensitive journalism or African journalism, it is critical that we also look at the history of the media in Africa within three historical contexts – precolonial, colonial, and postcolonial – and distinguish between media development in Anglophone and Francophone countries. In the precolonial context, our argument seeks to demolish the assertion that African journalism is that of bandwagonism and mimicry by showing how African journalism was found in the oral tradition through poetry, music, and stories. In the colonial context, we argue that the brand of journalism employed was characterized by liberalism in Anglophone Africa, leading to the explosion of private media ownership, while that of Francophone Africa was largely restricted, leading to the development of state-owned media, giving little room for developing private media.

Therefore, the press in Anglophone Africa became more critical of government, assuming the watchdog role, while the press in Francophone Africa became little more than propagandistic media, which, in essence, echoed their oral traditional past in precolonial Africa. In this context, we interrogate the widely held perception by media scholars that there is no journalism practice in Africa informed by African values to argue for the reserved applicability, harbored by media scholars, about the suitability of liberal press as applied in the African context. Anglo-American model – the Western liberal-democratic model – is not a one-size-fits-all model calling for the careful integration in different geographical context and spaces.[12]

The question as to whether there was any form of journalism in Africa before the colonial era may sound more journalistic than academic but nevertheless a question worth pursuing if we are to get any closure about the true origins of journalism in Africa.[13] A precolonial legacy characterized by oral tradition, as mentioned earlier, characterizes black African media.[14] With the foregoing understanding, an argument can therefore be advanced that there was a form of journalism before the advent of colonialists in Africa. Folk culture and communal storytelling (griots) musicians, poets, and dancers played the role of modern day journalists where we see the concept of civil society groups as well as in general and organized public spheres.[15] The problem is that communication scholars have only begun looking critically at the media during colonialism overlooking precolonial orality (journalism) because that is when most systems of mass media were introduced, but the truth is that even though governments change, it does not directly mean older forms disappear.[16]

Therefore, the precolonial period is very important in this chapter because the African oral tradition that defined journalism during this time resonates with the myth of the African ruler as a spiritual symbol of a people, where social values were stressed through group orientation, continuity, harmony, and balance,[17] and these values should be carried through in the era of technology through ideas such as those of the Twitter *baraza* chaired by village elders and chiefs. The question that this often invokes is that an individual doesn't belong until the question of "who you are" is given meaning by association of where one is from and born of whom (familial/ancestral ties), bringing to the fore African worldview of *Ubuntu/Utu* (a central philosophy in defining news values in African peace journalism). "*Ubuntu* is an ancient African ethic, a cultural mindset that tries to capture the essence of what it is to be human. A person is a person through other people". I am human because I belong [to a certain community], I participate, I share."[18]

It is this *Ubuntu/Utu* "African worldview, largely based on group solidarity and belonging, that largely informs the oral discourse style of journalism unique to pre-colonial Africa."[19] This orality through local language is what community radio and social media forums or *barazas* resurrects, while the former uses vocal codes, the latter boasts authentic local content generated from the local context, which is not only limited to texts but also includes sound and pictures and therefore, to some extent, also constitutes orality. The oral tradition as a form of communication and journalism presupposes the construction of reality in social context echoing cultural studies approach to media studies[20] initially developed in studying the 19th-century American press and, later, the British press. This kind of journalism is largely partisan attached to the nationalistic struggle following the end of Second World War. "Very much like the nationalist Africa press, the 19th century news of American press, and later British press tended to be reported by a great variety of people, often in first person and often through chronological narratives that stressed the participation of ordinary people."[21] News became news and more important because it was related to people (communal belonging) due to the conventions of associational journalism such as the following:

1 Eyewitness accounts make for the most newsworthy and authoritative stories.
2 A news story ought to be reported in the first person, or, where appropriate, in the third person.
3 The more firsthand accounts of events a newspaper provides its readers with, the better, even if some of those accounts contradict the political views of the editor or of one another.
4 Events ought to be reported chronologically, as they happen in real time with their significance determined by the number of people involved.

African oral discourse model of journalism, like oral praise poetry, is very useful, but they need to be appreciated cautiously due to their propagandistic nature characterized by praise-singing that has often led to partisan and ethnic journalism or journalism of belonging and eventually polarization and ethnicization of the press. The latter is nothing to celebrate for it is written on the wall how that kind of journalism has betrayed project Kenya from the early 1990s to landmark years such as 2007, 2013, and 2017 following ethnically disputed elections. This journalism was unique to Ivory Coast and the Cameroonian press. "The lack of distancing journalist from the audience makes it difficult for the press to assume a critical, neutral posture in their reporting. Thus the reporter, subject and audience end up forming a larger whole."[22] In the postcolonial period, most African journalists, including the propagandistic Francophone press, reverted to watchdog role to try to fit it in the wave that tried to shape nationalism in Africa. Here, we see journalism critical of the establishment even as they are affiliated and attached to the community in a polarized fashion.[23] Postcolonial press in East Africa is characterized by this kind of polarity, especially in countries like Kenya and Uganda; however, the press plays a watchdog role against the government and has often fallen victim of its harsh criticisms through repressive media laws and contentious ones, as explained in Chapter 7 by Jacinta Mwende, and journalists have often lost their lives through forced disappearances as witnessed in Kenya most recently.

This chapter contends that when models such as the civil society perspective that leans toward grassroots participation (as applied in Southern Africa) are integrated with oral discourse model of journalism, made possible through community radio and social media, to adapt to its liberal counterpart through Western peace journalism, then a hybrid model can emerge (African peace journalism) in a way that will improve journalism on the continent in the context of conflict, peace and security. This chapter, however, acknowledges that it is indeed difficult to radically transform postcolonial commercial media institutions that are there to sell cultural products for profits, and so the journalistic transformation called on would be one that begins from training in academic institutions of higher learning, bottom-up community youth outreach programs and to that of training practicing journalists in the newsrooms, as well as engaging citizens in other forms of media combinations like those conceptualized in this chapter (community radio and social media), for conflict transformation and peacebuilding in Kenya

Rationalizing the approach

The rationale proposed here borrows from an existing ToT infrastructure in peace and security in Kenya. The World Bank-funded Crime and Violence Prevention Training (CVPT) program, for example, which includes United States International University Africa, Kenya School of Government, Nairobi and National Crime Research Center, as well as the Center for Media, Democracy, Peace, and Security, Rongo University (incorporated later), has proved successful over the past few years since its inception in 2011 in the counties that it has been integrated. The program recognizes the relationship between crime and violence in Kenya in an effort to reduce the vacuum in and the lack of sophistication in crime and violence prevention through a paradigm shift that changes the perception of who is responsible for security and crime and violence prevention. CVPT has focused on capacity building through, first and foremost, conducting a baseline survey to identify prevalent crime and violence issues and applying the concept of crime and violence triangle to explain factors that are qualified as enablers of crime (opportunity, desire, and ability). CVPT and ToT have, so far, been done in order to replicate the ideas through multistakeholder grassroots engagement. This approach has, so far, proved to be reliable, but its sustainability level is still in question in the long term. For crime and violence to be prevented, there ought to be continuous engagement with a focus on the output orientation of grassroots community initiatives owned by the community that target the perpetrators and victims of conflict, crime, and violence and, at the same time, on mapping and tackling emerging conflict, crime, and violence typologies head-on. This is the gap that community and social media technologies fill.

As already observed, one of the most important but often neglected institutions in conflict prevention in the peace and security architecture is the media. Given that typically, the profiling of conflict in Kenya points to youth demographics variables where the youth are perceived as the perpetrators and or victims of conflict for obvious reasons, some of which are captured in the Crime and Violence Triangle concept it comes as good news that the youth are the biggest users of technology and social media platforms meaning that they stand a chance to benefit through training. The crime and violence prevention concept is therefore very useful in broadening the debate about conflict and peacebuilding in the North Rift.

With the onset of devolution and that ushered in decentralized governance, there has been a surge of community radio stations whose potential can be tapped and deliberately used for conflict prevention. At the moment, the community stations are not being utilized for conflict prevention, and neither are they being fully exploited in conflict resolution and peacebuilding. In this chapter, as pointed out earlier, we are arguing that conducting a module on community radio for conflict resolution and peacebuilding training is crucial, followed by piloting and establishing existing community radio stations in the North Rift and using them for peacebuilding and conflict resolution. The mapped community radio stations would thus be used as the entry point to spread peacebuilding training and output-oriented interventions in counties in the North Rift.

Furthermore, as opposed to material interventions to peace and security employed by the state, such as military deployment, arbitrary arrests, curfews and forced disappearance to deal with conflicts, community radio and social media for peacebuilding proposed by the Center for Media, Democracy, Peace, and Security, Rongo University, is a softer philosophical media institutional and practical approach that uses a methodology that has more of a chance of success in solving conflicts and security challenges through constructive community radio dialogues.

It is through this radio space (public sphere) that community members can deliberate and engage in uncomfortable dialogues in conflict issues affecting them in the North Rift and how to prevent, mitigate or solve them. However, we recognize that community radio alone is not a one-stop shop for peacebuilding, and therefore, we recommend going beyond community radio stations to include social media. Social media, due to its user-generated content and interactivity, has the potential of complementing community radio stations. For example, users of social media can connect to community radio hotlines to report conflicts and crime or to send distress and peace messages in cases of conflict. Social media can be the most effective tool for peace mobilization and interactive discussions that are geared toward conflict resolution. In this approach, the objectives ought to be clear and clearly stated. Some of the objectives of community radio and social media approach for peacebuilding in the North Rift would be the following:

1   To integrate North Rift community radio and social media for peacebuilding into development programs
2   To mainstream community radio, social media, and peacebuilding training in county government in the North Rift
3   To practically contribute to peacebuilding through community radio and social media in North Rift
4   To map existing community radio stations in the North Rift and most utilized social media spaces to explore their potential for peacebuilding
5   To sensitize the community on how to explore social media for peacebuilding through pan-African journalistic philosophies of *Utu*, *Umoja*, and *Harambee*.

Community radio, social media, and the idea of user-generated content are important platforms in stimulating grassroots dialogues. The connections between the media and peacebuilding in East Africa should be owned by the people who should strive to tell the story creatively for peacebuilding and sustainable development. The idea of using African lenses to peacebuilding and conflict reporting through mediated orality is a refreshing path toward transformative journalism in Africa by imbibing pan-African institutional methodological approaches and Africa philosophies of *Utu* (humanity), *Umoja* (unity), and *Harambee* (collective responsibility) as news values as opposed to copy-and-paste journalism that leads to sensationalism and thus the escalation of conflict in the continent. These new approached are discussed in details in Chapter 4.

Approach

A baseline survey entry strategy can seek to answer the following questions: Who are the perpetrators of conflict in the North Rift? Can the perpetrators be pointed out clearly? What are their composition, structure, and philosophy? Who are their collaborators and sympathizers? Who are their financiers? What is the political angle of conflict? What is the role of politicians? Which community stations do we have in counties in the North Rift? What is the role of community radio stations and social media in conflict prevention and peacebuilding? What social media platforms do community members in the North Rift frequent? How can community members use such a platform to generate content for peacebuilding? These questions will help unravel the origins of conflict, whether or not there are structured weaknesses in the North Rift counties' coordination framework, and, finally, establish whether there is a coherent prevention strategy that has been rolled out and map out other beneficial programs in the long and short term.

Community radio and social media for conflict resolution and peacebuilding

Mainstreaming conflict resolution and peacebuilding in counties in the North Rift through short media literacy training courses is critical. These courses should target county communication officials and community radio station media practitioners. In this approach, research content from the baseline survey can be integrated in the counties through short training courses conducted in government institutions and institutions of higher learning, such as the Kenya School of Government and the Center for Media, Democracy, Peace, and Security, Rongo University, to create awareness on the role of community radio and social media for peacebuilding and conflict resolution. The community radio course can focus on how to use radio content effectively for peacebuilding and conflict resolution. Practically, this means a mix of call-in shows and mini-documentaries targeting different segments of the audience with the following output-oriented content/narrative:

1 Community-driven interventions in conflict resolution and peacebuilding
2 Expert interviews and studio discussion from experts or studio invited guests on the role of the community and other stakehold ers in conflict resolution and peacebuilding
3 Call-in shows and social media (Facebook, WhatsApp, or Instagram) studio messages on peacebuilding and conflict resolution
4 Telephone hotlines for reporting conflicts and distress calls in times of conflict

The social media approach will include community sensitization on citizen journalism through pan-African philosophies of *Utu, Umoja*, and *Harambee*, as discussed in detail in Chapter 4.

Measuring output and conclusion

The success of the program could be measured by the changing perception of callers in call-in shows, reduced incidences of reported crime and violence in police stations, reduced reported deaths and injuries in county hospitals due to insecurity and conflict, youth success stories of engaging in progressive activities in the community, community and citizen engagement and interest in conflict resolution and peacebuilding, increased exposure and awareness of conflict prevention and peacebuilding radio content in the community, and active student enrollment and engagement in media literacy courses.

Conflict is part and parcel of African societies and is a necessary step for community evolution and progress; however, it ought to be controlled in civilized societies. Conflicts prevalent in the North Rift region are undermining socioeconomic and political progress in that region and are threatening devolution. As counties in the North Rift work jointly to form an economic block, conflict becomes one of the biggest threats to achieving their objectives of shared prosperity, poverty alleviation, and unity. It is therefore crucial that creative solutions be implemented to solve conflict, crime, and violence in this region to create a good environment for investments.

In this chapter, we argue that the Center for Media, Democracy, Peace, and Security, Rongo University, in concert with partners such as the Kenya School of Government, with its crime and violence prevention infrastructure, and others recommend a combined methodology of using community radio and social media for conflict resolution through pan-African journalism. The community radio and social media approach has the local content advantage (local language) and individual drive through user-generated content and thus allows for greater success and ownership. Due to the technical capabilities of both technologies, there is also wider reach and a great potential in solving emerging conflicts, crime, and violence through distress calls, resource mobilization, and community sensitization for posterity.

Notes

1 Fredrick Ogenga, "'Africanizing' Media Coverage of Threats to Peace and Security," *Kujenga Amani*, 2016.
2 John Oluoch, "Re-Situating Vernacular Media: A Tool for Peace Building Among the Abakuria in Kenya in Africa Peace Journalism – A Manual for Media Practitioners in East Africa," *Rongo University's Center for Media, Democracy, Peace and Security and Social Science Research Council's Africa Peacebuilding Network Regional Peace Journalism Training Workshop*, Great Lakes Hotel, Kisumu, 16–17 March 2017.
3 John Oluoch, "Re-Situating Vernacular Media"; Fredrick Ogenga, "The Role of the Kenyan Media in the 2007 Elections," *EISA Journal of African Election* 7, no. 2 (2008): 124–134.
4 Fredrick Ogenga, "The Role of the Kenyan Media in the 2007 Elections".
5 Messanga Obama, "Normativity and the Problem of Look in the Emergence of Citizen Journalism," *Advances in Journalism and Communication* 4, no. 1 (1996): 1–7.
6 Fredrick Ogenga, "The Role of the Kenyan Media in the 2007 Elections".
7 John Oluoch, "Re-Situating Vernacular Media".
8 John Oluoch, "Re-Situating Vernacular Media".
9 Fredrick Ogenga, "Youth Engagement for Peacebuilding Through Street Film, Campus, Peace Ambassadors and Community Radio for Peace," *IDRS Stakeholder Workshop*, Nairobi, 1–3 March 2017.
10 Duncan Omanga, "Chiefstaincy in the Social Media Space," *International Journal of Security and Development* 10, no. 3 (2015): 67–82, www.stability journal.org/articles/10.5334/sta.eq Accessed 15 May 2018.
11 Guncan Omanga, "Chiefstaincy in the Social Media Space".
12 Ibrahim Shaw, "Towards an African Journalism Model: A Critical Historical Perspective," *International Communication Gazette* 71, no. 6 (2009): 491–510.
13 Ibrahim Shaw, "Towards an African Journalism Model: A Critical Historical Perspective".

14 L. M. Bourgault, *Mass Media in Sub-Saharan Africa* (Bloomington: Indiana University Press, 1995).
15 Shaw, "Towards an African Journalism Model: A Critical Historical Perspective".
16 Bourgault, *Mass Media in Sub-Saharan Africa*.
17 Bourgault, *Mass Media in Sub-Saharan Africa*.
18 Shaw, "Towards an African Journalism Model: A Critical Historical Perspective," 496.
19 Shaw, "Towards an African Journalism Model: A Critical Historical Perspective," 496.
20 W. Onge, *Orality and Literacy: The Technologizing of the World* (London: Methuen, 1982).
21 Shaw, "Towards an African Journalism Model: A Critical Historical Perspective" 496.
22 Bourgault, *Mass Media in Sub-Saharan Africa*, 18.
23 F. B. Nyamnjoh, *Africa's Media: Democracy and the Politics of Belonging* (London and New York: UNISA Press, 2005).

4 Hybrid Peace Journalism

Institutional philosophical approaches to peace and security in Africa

Fredrick Ogenga

This chapter argues that the way in which the media represents terrorism could be a contributing factor to the rising number of cases of violent extremism in a country. Media scholars are faced with the burden of assessing the potential impacts of providing wide coverage to acts of terrorism, which is arguably a way that the media could be aiding terror through the publicity it affords terrorist attacks based on its breaking-news approach. This approach can be contrasted with other methods that give terrorism a media blackout, although this could inadvertently lead to more violent attacks by terrorists to make the point that media boycotts cannot deter them.

Kenya has experienced a surge of terrorism, with the main attacks occurring at the Westgate Mall, Garissa University, Mpeketoni, and Mandera. These major attacks were often interspersed with smaller attacks that had similar devastating consequences. The main questions this chapter poses are, To what extent should the Kenyan media cover terrorist attacks? and What are the likely consequences of providing little or no coverage of terrorist attacks? This chapter argues that peace journalism provides an appropriate frame for determining the extent to which terrorism should be covered by the media in Kenya. Peace journalism strives to tell the truth about conflicting parties in a fair and objective manner with the overall aim of resolving the conflict by balancing the perspectives of all the parties involved. However, due to contextual factors, peace journalism should be applied in Africa in a manner that responds to local dynamics.

This chapter proposes a departure from the Western sensationalism that currently characterizes terrorism news coverage in Africa. This approach, based on core Pan-African principles, is conceptualized as Hybrid Peace Journalism (HPJ). HPJ urges journalists to deliberately mention the word *peace* when reporting on terrorism and to avoid stereotyping and inflammatory labels such as "Islamic terrorist," "Muslim terrorist," "Islamic jihadist" and "Somali terrorist" in their news coverage. However, the media uses such words partly because the local educational institutions that train journalists rely on mainstream traditional Western conceptualizations of news and news values. This approach demands that news has to be sensational such that "if it bleeds, it leads." It is therefore useful for African institutions and scholars to reconceptualize the approach toward the training of journalists and the practice of journalism in Africa. Such a new approach should be context-sensitive and rich in African values, particularly those relating to peace, for journalists to integrate African peace-centered perspectives when covering acts of terrorism.

Thinking about an African-centered media

The media in Africa is heavily influenced by Western values and paradigms. Kenyan media, for example, has been commercially structured, often serving the interest of audiences, owners, and advertisers.[1] Historically, the Kenyan media has not occupied a comfortable space regarding the political, economic, technological and social environment.[2] They have simply acted as the mouthpiece of the government. Therefore, before we think of an African-centered media and how Africa is represented by media reports on terrorism, we must first explore a number of works that have made significant contributions to the literature about the Western media representation of Africa. Examples include the works of V. Y. Mudimbe, Ali Mazrui, Francis B. Nyamnjoh and Milton Allimadi.[3] Mudimbe's compelling works, *The Invention of Africa* and *The Idea of Africa*, have made significant contributions to the critique of the construction of otherness in Western discourses and the assumption that Western epistemology about ideas of Africa and its people is an authoritative blueprint. In *The Invention of Africa*, Mudimbe hypothesizes the possibility of authentic African systems of knowledge that are not necessarily bound by the normative conventions of Western science defined through a certain episteme. Mudimbe brings about the idea of "gnosis," derived from the Greek word *gnosko*, which means seeking to know, inquiry, methods of knowing, investigations or acquaintance with someone. He describes gnosis that is bound by African traditionalism and ways of reasoning, which are different and unique from the Western episteme. He argues that

> [o]ften the word [*gnosis*] is used in a more specialized sense, that of higher and esoteric knowledge, but one strictly under the control of specific procedures for its use as well as transmission. *Gnosis* is, consequently, different from *doxa* or opinion, and, on the other

hand, cannot be confused by episteme understood as both science and general intellectual configuration.[4]

Mudimbe's title *The Invention of Africa* is therefore "a methodological tool that embraces the question of what is and what is not African philosophy, and orients the debate in another direction by focusing on the possibility of philosophy as part of the larger body of knowledge of Africa called 'Africanism.'"[5] In conceptualizing such a possibility, Mudimbe questions the authenticity of the subjects of such discourses that can be regarded as "real African" and are informed by African gnosis. Who has the moral authority to represent or talk about an African discourse? Who has the right and credentials to produce it, describe it, or comment about it? Is it African scholars of philosophy or scholars of African philosophy? And what does their contribution mean to African philosophy? The former have been instrumental in the rejection of the Hobbesian "man in the bush" myth by separating the "real" African from the Westernized African and solely relying on the first. However, their efforts have often been insufficient because they have failed to explain African philosophy beyond the parameters of conventional Western epistemology and normative conventions. Consequently, Mudimbe looks upstream with caution for answers to precisely what makes such an objective African reality possible, while regarding "discourses on African societies, cultures, and peoples as signs of something else."

So, if the media is reporting on terrorism in Africa, what kind of discourses, angles, and frames should they use? Mudimbe's approach reveals the level of caution required by journalists reporting on terrorism in Africa. Arguably, the Western media has been responsible for setting the pattern for how global media frames and covers terrorism. Domestic politics in Western countries had an outsized impact on the discourse around what constitutes terrorism and who is a terrorist, leading to some nations being branded the "axis of evil" by George W. Bush's administration. This approach labeled certain countries exporters of radical Islamism, primarily Iran, Syria, Afghanistan, Libya, Somalia, and Sudan.

These countries are at the core of US president Donald Trump's controversial new immigration executive order which attempts to suspend immigration from these nations to the United States for up to 90 days. This policy has been viewed by many observers as a blanket ban on certain Muslim countries, which frames immigrant Muslims from Africa and the Middle East as potential terrorists. Such policies are informed by the Western empirical episteme. Trump's executive order, though successfully challenged in court, partly explains how easily local paro-chial politics can shape wider global public opinion. It also raises questions as to the place of African voices and engagement in this ide-ological struggle revolving around the power to define threats posed by terrorism (and to whom).

Paulin J. Hountondji's 1996 book, *African Philosophy, Myth and Reality*, seems to echo the weakness of African philosophy, a term which she boldly refers to as a myth. After mentioning several scholars of African philosophy on the continent, including those inspired by Christianity – such as Placide Tempels, Alexis Kagame, Mgr Makara-kiza and Antoine Mabona – and several other authors, such as Kwame Nkrumah, Leopold Senghor, Adebayo Adesanya, and William Abra-ham, Hountondji concludes that these scholars have "projected onto [African traditions and oral literature] their own philosophical beliefs hoping to enhance their credibility."[6] Hountondji is convinced that the brand of philosophy masquerading as authentic, collective, and homogeneous African philosophy is actually a personal philosophy. She argues:

> That is how the functioning of this thesis of a collective African philosophy works: It is a smoke screen behind which each author is able to manipulate his own philosophical views. It has noth-ing beyond this ideological function: It is indeterminate discourse with no object . . . it is therefore clear [for example] that the Bantu philosophy of the one is not the philosophy of the Bantu but that of Tempels, that the Bantu-Rwandais philosophy of the other is not that of the Rwandais but that of Kagame.[7]

Nevertheless, the most interesting issue is how Hountondji conceptu-alizes African philosophy. She introduces the idea of speaking of Afri-can philosophy in a new sense arguing that

> [w]e must draw a line between African and non-African writers [journalists], not because one category is better than the other, or because both might not, in the last analysis say the same thing, but because the subject being African philosophy, we cannot exclude a geographical variable taken here as empirical, contingent, extrin-sic to the content or significance to the discourse and as quite apart from any questions of theoretical connections.[8]

From the preceding perspective, although the works of authors such as Placide Tempels (mentioned earlier) deal with an African subject and have played a significant or "decisive role in African ethnophilosophy," they belong to European scientific literature "in the same way as anthropology in general, although it deals with non-Western societies, is an embodiment of Western science, no more and no less."[9] Therefore, according to Hountondji, what makes the works of authors like Mudimbe critical is that they have emanated from the perspective of an African writer. However, they have also been criticized for assuming that there is an "inherent centrism of the Western episteme in all representations of Africa (even African ones)."[10] However, these works have often been credited for carving out possible pathways for African philosophy "beyond the impasse between ethnophilosophy and adaptation of Western philosophy to Africa." Mudimbe's works are important because they analyze the representation of Africa in the Western discourse and by African scholars. What narratives do media in Africa construct when reporting on terrorism on the continent and what intellectual positions do African scholars assume when researching terrorism, including how terrorism is reported by the media in Africa and African media?

The most interesting point in the debate is how Africa is conceptualized in the West as the weaker partner in the war on terrorism, compelling countries like Kenya to "copy and paste" an American-style antiterrorism approach in dealing with al-Shabaab in spite of the fact that it falls short on some aspects of the human rights compliancy test. As a result, sensational reports on terrorist attacks in Kenya have fed mass anxiety and undermined the security situation in the country.

Francis B. Nyamnjoh argues that the assumptions underpinning African journalistic practices are not informed by the fact that Africans should be involved in Africanizing their modernity and modernizing their Africanity. Therefore, a complex narrative that goes far beyond the simplistic Western one regarding Africa is necessary. This is not to assume that there is a homogeneity about the best ways of being and doing to which all Africans should aspire as they walk into modernity and civilization. The confusion about what is African and what is Western is at the heart of the dilemma currently facing journalism in Africa, which should strive toward creatively approaching African affairs with great sensitivity and nuance.[11]

Therefore, African journalists operate in a world where everything has been pre-described for them by others and their only duty is to put these into practice without the opportunity to rethink and reinvent them. Nyamnjoh claims that if journalism privileges a hierarchy of humanity and human creativity and that the latter in Africa is presumed to be in an abyss, then such journalism is bound to be prescriptive, condescending, contrived, caricatured, and hardly in tune with the quest by Africa for equality, recognition, and representation.

The same argument can be applied to the "War on Terror" in Africa, where a closer inspection shows how journalism has been comprehending and articulating reality through the lenses of those who are convinced that their superior ideas should be uncritically adopted by those from developing contexts.[12]

Mudimbe quotes the French Anthropologist Jean-Loup Amselle in an interesting analysis that brings forth the possibility of unity among varying discourses, a central premise of the HPJ conceptualization. Amselle's work, written in French, includes a collection of nine essays that introduce another form of "reason" founded on the basis of the quest for truth in multicultural societies. This kind of reason is less concerned with differences (distinction) and questions of what concepts existed first. Rather, it establishes the manner in which differences are integrated to form a totality that is universal. Amselle undermines the tension related to questions about the universality of democracy by expressing views sympathetic to cultural relativism (cultural empathy) and questioning ethno-philosophy and ethnocentrism.[13]

Amselle presents a rationality that "refuses to reduce African culture and the body of its social practices and negotiations to an immobile essence" and, at the same time, gives a critical appraisal of the politics of universality.[14] Mudimbe quotes Melville Herskovits who states "when one pays attention to the declension of the concept of civilization and culture in the singular and the plural; the singular always postulates the unity of humankind, the plural its diversity and cultural variation."[15] Tensions that often manifest themselves in brutal acts of terrorism are as a result of the global clash of identity and tension between cultural homogeneity and heterogeneity.

Herskovits quotes Foucault to illustrate how "Western culture has contributed to the name of man, a being who, by one and the same interplay of reasons, must be a positive domain of knowledge and cannot be an object of science." Such views are central in questioning ethnocentrism in order to give room for cultural diversity. Culture approached in its diversity presents humanity with perhaps the best possibility of finding closure to the ever-present question of "objective truth" that would speak well to the collective predicament of mankind and bury terrorism in the dump of history.

The argument by Herskovits captures the discourse guiding the HPJ philosophical approach discussed in the next subsection. Herskovits argues that

[t]he very core of cultural relativism is the social discipline that comes out of respect for differences – of mutual respect. Emphasis of the worth of many ways of life not one, is the affirmation of values in each culture. Such values seek to understand and to harmonize goals, not to judge and destroy those that do not dovetail with our own. Cultural history teaches that, important as it is to discern and study the parallelism in human civilizations, it is no less important to discern and study the different ways man has devised to fulfill his needs.[16]

HPJ

HPJ is an Africanized version of Galtung and Mari Holmboe Ruge's concept of peace journalism (good journalism) that seeks to look at conflicts in Africa with African lenses and wisdom or "gnosis" for peace and security to avoid the escalation of violent conflicts.[17] Peace journalism enables editors and reporters to make good choices, including how to frame stories and carefully choose which words are used to create an atmosphere conducive for peace and supportive of peace initiatives and peacemakers, without compromising the basic principles of good or ethical journalism.[18]

The core elements of HPJ are research, training, and practice. The research component entails focusing on pan-African methodologies and concepts that reflect both contextual differentiation and conceptual precision. This involves answering questions about how we should apply peace journalism in Africa given the contextual realities and whether or not journalistic values such as "if it bleeds it leads" are precisely applied in conflict reporting and reports on terrorism in Africa. The training component addresses the challenge of transforming mainstream media institutions from within due to their long tradition of commercializing news content. News, to many media houses, is stories that must "sell" in order for them to sustain their operations and make a profit. This implies that a younger generation of journalists needs to be trained so they can master the newly formulated pan-African HPJ approach to news reporting that incorporates the African values of *Utu*, *Umoja*, and *Harambee* into conflict reporting. Furthermore, trained journalists and media practitioners are expected to practically apply these principles, which leads to the third component: practice.

The approach calls for the use of "Campus Community Radio for Peacebuilding" managed by students or "Campus Peace Ambassadors." These community radio stations will play two roles: first, they will

Peace Journalism   =   **Good Journalism**

Good Journalism (West)   Universal Attribute (African Gnosis)

HBRID PEACE
JORNALISM (HPJ)

Departure from
Conflict Reporting

Peace Reporting

Development
Oriented

Negative Peace; prevents
conflicts
Positive peace; tolerance,
Godly Peace

Figure 4.1 Hybrid Peace Journalism Institutional Model for Peace and Security
in Africa PREMISE

act as training facilities for upcoming journalists. Second, they will be
used as peacebuilding spaces for addressing peace and security issues
such as conflict, youth radicalization, and violent extremism. This will
enable young people to exit violence, learn to explore various types of
peacebuilding, and nurture resilient communities through action learning. This underscores the salience of institutional training in universities on news reporting and peace-centered news coverage in Africa.

Media, terrorism, and peacebuilding in Africa

Terrorism has been defined differently by different scholars but the
master narrative of what constitutes terrorism has been constructed
by the media. Much of what the media has relied on is the idea of

negativity and sensationalism, a representation strategy that has been exported to Africa for covering incidences of terrorism. This is reminiscent of the manner in which Africa has generally been negatively represented by the Western media.[19] The narrative about the continent has been dominated by references to disease, failed states, poverty, and conflicts. However, the question is, Who is responsible for the invention of this negative narrative about Africa?

While poverty and disease are largely perceived as an African problem, the case of terrorism is more complicated. This is because while the historical trajectory of the African continent reminds us of colonialism and slavery, which are arguably forms of terrorism, Africa is historically littered with narratives about Africans terrorizing their own during territorial expansions and inter-ethnic conflicts. More recently, identity conflicts sanctioned by the state and civilians have taken place, such as the 2007 and 2017 postelection violence in Kenya and the 1994 genocide in Rwanda. However, the notion of terrorism in Africa is largely "foreign" and can be quickly traced from colonial struggles that gave birth to nationalist movements and nationalist media agitating for freedom. It was also not unusual for colonial authorities to label nationalist/liberation movements such as Mau Mau of Kenya, Maji Maji of Tanzania, and Umkhonto we Sizwe in South Africa as "terrorists." Is there a way Africa can reclaim its historicity in the context of such dominant negative representations? Scholars would premise their arguments on the role of colonialism and slavery; colonialism contributed largely to the negative discourse and the idea of the "dark continent" as explorers and missionaries scrambled for a piece of Africa under the guise of "enlightening" the natives. It is the extension of this narrative, as advanced by the local and foreign media, which would compel keen observers to have quick answers and conclusions to the reasons behind the negative representation of Africa.

The Kenyan press has often presented news about terrorism in an alarming manner, often using bold headlines, red colors to indicate terror hot spots, and graphic images of the extent of damage immediately after terrorist attacks. This is well illustrated by the *Daily Nation* of July 9, 2015, when the statistics on casualties of terrorism in Kenya were displayed prominently using bold front-page headlines and graphic images of victims carried in body bags by the Red Cross rescue teams. The article uses a map of Kenya to illustrate ungovernable spaces between Kenya and Somalia – apparently due to al-Shabaab attacks – in red, symbolic of the chaotic situation there. Kenyans largely rely on mainstream newspapers for accurate information to help them come to terms with serious events affecting the country, such as terrorism. This is not to argue that if the media stops publicizing terrorism terrorists will not attack. Terrorists may still attack even with limited or no media coverage. It may be argued that media blackouts could potentially incite them to unleash even more sophisticated, organized, and devastating attacks just to prove a point.

When covering terrorism, it is important for journalists to be exercise caution in deciding, for example, what pictures to use and how to frame stories to avoid spreading fear among the public, who should otherwise be encouraged to remain resilient in order to overcome terror. The media plays a crucial role in shaping perceptions and attitudes towards terrorism and security.[20] In his essay titled "Reporting Terrorism among Kenyan Media: Should Journalists be Cautious?" Abraham Kisang argues that the media should deny terrorists the opportunity to access publicity.[21] By framing dramatic events of terror to attract large audiences and failing to detach themselves from terrorism stories, journalists actually praise people known or suspected to be al-Shabaab members while giving relatively little media coverage to counterterrorism measures.

CMDPS HPJ institutional approach

It is in the context of the foregoing that the Center for Media, Democracy, Peace, and Security (CMDPS) at Rongo University launched a new graduate program in Media, Democracy, Peace, and Security and a Visiting Post-Doctoral Fellowship Program based on peace journalism (as conceptualized by its proponents). In addition, CMDPS has institutionalized a new philosophical approach to peace journalism research in Africa by developing HPJ based on news values inspired by *Utu*, *Umoja*, and *Harambee*. The basic tenets of HPJ can be gleaned from Fredrick Ogenga's 2015 article in the *African Journal of Democracy and Governance*. It is developmentally driven by African ideals of community belonging (*Ujamaa*), unity (*Harambee/Umoja*), and humanity (*Utu/Ubuntu*). The media has a moral obligation to be true to the local context and nuance and to participate and stand up for peace.[22] The HPJ approach has also been integrated into an ongoing global project on exiting violence.

This kind of journalism calls for peace, love, and unity, imbibing the character of the great African forefathers and their dreams about the future of the continent. A future blessed by positive peace, tranquility, and prosperity for all. The focus is on peace because it is a prerequisite for development, something that Africa direly needs. To practically introduce HPJ, the center conducted a "Peace and Reconciliation Journalism Project" in partnership with the Center for Global Peace Jour nalism at Park University (USA) and Ugwe FM (now Radio Rameny) to train practicing radio journalists in the region on peace reporting. It is important to educate practicing journalists in regions of Africa where terror is rife on how to report terrorism using HPJ principles that take into account the complexities of local sociocultural, political, and economic dynamics.

HPJ methodology and practice

The CMDPS is working with other partners, including the Peacemaker Association (USA) and its Kenyan chapter, the Peacemaker Corps Foundation Kenya to invest in the power of radio (Campus Community Radio for Peacebuilding). The latter is to be run by CMDPS Hybrid Peace Journalism Club members. The members are undergraduate students pursuing communication, journalism, and media studies. The Peacemaker Foundation Kenya and Peacemakers Association (USA) are currently working on developing a film, TV, and radio (internet) academy for peacebuilding in Kisumu, Kenya, where students will be trained in various skills on how to use technology for peacebuilding and to support an ongoing annual event called "The Global Peace in the Streets Film Festival" that takes place at the UN Headquarters in New York as part of the foundation's Economic and Social Council Status responsibility with the UN.

What is terrorism?

There is no single definition for terrorism.[23] The problem of defining terrorism has hindered its analysis since the inception of terrorism studies in the early 1970s. In his definition of terrorism, Max Abrahms takes the "strategic model" view, the dominant paradigm in terrorism studies which posits that terrorists are rational actors who attack civilians for political ends.[24] However, there is no denying that the media has often played a role in constructing what appears to be the definition of terrorism.[25] Today's freedom fighters are tomorrow's terrorists; examples include the Irish Republican Army, the anticolonial Mau Mau movement in Kenya, Umkhonto we Sizwe (the armed wing of the Africa National Congress), the Islamic Resistance Movement (Hamas), and the Palestinian National Liberation Movement (Fatah). Traditional case studies on the media and terrorism, though few, have focused on the symbiotic relationship between the media and terrorism based on the assumption that media often increases the risk of terrorism because terrorism is used as a communication mechanism by political extremists.[26]

Citizens' risk perception and attitudes toward terrorism and insecurity

In a study on the perception of terrorism and security and the role of the media, Petra Guatsi and Zdenka Mansfeldova pose three very important questions that can help us understand the centrality of the media in understanding terrorism: How does the media frame terrorism and organized crime? Has the media coverage of terrorism and organized crime made the public more sensitive to the issue of security? And if so, how are the (security) threats perceived and discussed by the media?[27] The widespread publication of information about threats to national security, the reactions of governments, and steps taken to prosecute offenders clearly demonstrates that more security does not necessarily make society happier. Happiness is connected to not only the feeling of safety and absence of fear but also the absence of far-reaching security mechanisms that infringe on the privacy and freedom of citizens. This helps in explaining the tensions between security and freedom and the moral cost of security in terms of sacrificing individual privacy.[28] The media, being at the forefront of shaping perceptions and attitudes, can provide outlets for whistleblowers and act as a watchdog for civil liberties and privacy in this era of the global war on terrorism. The question citizens must ask is how much security do they want and at what price. The media therefore plays a critical role as an arena where information is made available and negotiated and where opinions, including those of terrorists, are formed. The media therefore has a role to play when it comes to risk perception, political communication, and the tensions between freedom and security that would affect terrorism and responses to it in one way or the other.[29]

Guatsi and Mansfeldova argue that higher risk perception increases political intolerance, ethnocentrism, xenophobia, and prejudice. One can point to the increasingly common belief in Kenya that Somalis and Muslims are terrorists. Similar considerations have informed new immigration laws in the United States and Europe concerning refugees and foreigners. It should be noted that threat perception reduces cognitive abilities and leads to closed-mindedness, intolerance to difference, or those considered as the "other."

The primary focus of terrorism is political communication intended to persuade the target audience to pursue some form of action intended to achieve some political ends. This is why audiences are critical in terrorism. How effectively audiences will be influenced by terrorism as a means of political communication will therefore depend to some extent on how the media frames that communication and how this matches with their level of security risk perception (both individual and collective/national) or fear vis-à-vis individual citizens' willingness to surrender their freedom as the price for security. This is why some have argued that the global war on terror is just another excuse for espionage, allowing elites to control the masses who surrender their own liberty and privacy at the altar of security surveillance, which will never make a society happy and peaceful.

There have been studies, such as Dominic Rohner and Bruno Frey's, which have focused on testing whether or not media coverage increases the risk of terrorism.[30] Others have focused on the relationship among terrorism, religion, and ethnicity; the economics of terrorism and the "common interest game"; and the psychological impacts of terrorism.[31]

In addition, most studies focusing on terrorism in Africa, such as Wanjiru Kamau's "Kenya and the War on Terrorism" and Jeremy Pres-dtholt's "Kenya, the United States, and Counterterrorism" have emphasized the sociocultural and political implications of counterterrorism with minimal reference to literature on media and terrorism.[32] Ogenga's 2012 study goes further to interrogate media approaches to news that sanction representation of terrorist attacks, and therein terrorism.[33] This chapter explores the study of the media and terrorism by not only inspecting Western ideologies of journalism but also presenting an opportunity to reinvent journalism in Africa inspired by Africanism in the context of the new threat of terror in Africa.

Conclusion

The media in Kenya and African need to go beyond the superficial representation of terrorism. The ways in which Kenya's public discourse and mainstream print media have been representing terrorism could be partly responsible for the surge of violent extremism in the country. This chapter argues that such media representations are motivated by the absence of Africa-centric frameworks that can guide journalists working in the continent, especially those in conflict regions, on how to cover news in a manner that would cultivate dialogue and peace rather than fuel conflict. Unfortunately, news about terrorism is usually sensationalized making governments, policymakers, and audiences susceptible to mass anxiety or fear occasioned by such attacks.

In the spirit of the necessity of a more context-specific and peace-oriented framing, HPJ borrows from peace journalism as an ideological seedbed and fuses it with African traditions (gnosis) when covering news about terrorism or conflict. The argument is that since the media is central in political communication and is often used by terrorists for propaganda purposes, the same media can be used to forestall terrorism by spreading messages of hope, peace, love, and unity. HPJ is inspired by the latter and also assumes that conflict resolution and peacebuilding in Africa are preconditions for economic development, good governance, job creation, poverty alleviation, and investment in better health and education systems. As has been noted, these are the hallmarks of the "Africa Rising" narrative and Kenya's Vision 2030.

Notes

1 Nixon Kariithi, "The Crisis of Developing Journalism in Africa," *Media Development*, 4 (1994): 28–30.
2 Peter Oriare Mbeke, *The Media, Legal Regulatory and Policy Environment in Kenya: A Historical Briefing* (Nairobi: School of Journalism and Mass Communication, University of Nairobi, 2008).
3 Vumbi Yoka Mudimbe, *The Invention of Africa: Gnosis, Philosophy and the Order of Knowledge* (Bloomington and Indianapolis: Indiana University Press, 1988); V. Y. Mudimbe, *The Idea of Africa* (Bloomington and Indianapolis: Indiana University Press); Ali Mazrui, "The Re-invention of Africa: Edward Said, V. Y. Mudimbe and Beyond," *Research in African Literature* 36, no. 3 (2005): 68–82; Francis B. Nyamnjoh, *Africa's Media: Between Professional Ethics and Cultural Belonging* (Windhoek: Friedrich-Ebert-Stiftung, 2010); Milton Allimadi, *The Hearts of Darkness: How Whites Created the Racist Image of Africa* (New York: Black Star Books, 2002).
4 Vumbi Yoka Mudimbe, *The Invention of Africa*, ix.
5 Vumbi Yoka Mudimbe, *The Invention of Africa*, ix.
6 Paulin J. Hountondji, *African Philosophy: Myth and Reality* (Bloomington: Indiana University Press, 1996), 62.
7 Paulin Hountondji, *African Philosophy: Myth and Reality*, 62.
8 Paulin Hountondji, *African Philosophy: Myth and Reality*, 64.
9 Paulin Hountondji, *African Philosophy: Myth and Reality*, 64.
10 Kai Kresse, "Reading Mudimbe: An Introduction," *Journal of African Cultural Studies* 17, no. 1 (2005): 7.
11 Francis Nyamnjoh, *Africa's Media*.
12 Francis Nyamnjoh, *Africa's Media*, 15.
13 Vumbi Yoka Mudimbe, *The Idea of Africa*, 53.
14 Vumbi Yoka Mudimbe, *The Idea of Africa*, 53.
15 Vumbi Yoka Mudimbe, *The Idea of Africa*, 49.
16 Vumbi Yoka Mudimbe, *The Idea of Africa*, 49.
17 Johan Galtung and Mari Holmboe Ruge, "The Structure of Foreign News: The Presentation of the Congo, Cuba and Cyprus Crises in Four Norwegian Newspapers," *Journal of Peace Research* 2, no. 1 (1965): 64–90.
18 Jake Lynch and Annabel McGoldrick, *Peace Journalism* (Stroud, UK: Hawthorn Press, 2005).
19 Fredrick Ogenga, "Political-Economy of the Kenyan Media – Towards a Culture of Active Citizen Journalism," *Global Media Journal African Edition* 4,

no. 2 (2010): 151–162; Fredrik Ogenga, "Mugabe Must Go: Textual Meanings of the Representation of the Zimbabwean Situation by the South African Press," *Africa Conflict and Peace Building Review* 1, no. 1 (2011): 39–70; Fredrik Ogenga, "Is Peace Journalism Possible in the War Against Terror in Somalia? How the Kenyan Daily Nation and the Standard Represented Operation Linda Nchi," *Conflict and Communication Online* 11, no. 2 (2012): 1–14; Fredrik Ogenga, "Assessing Peace Journalism on Kenya Television Network's Diaspora Voices in the 2013 Elections," *Africa Journal of Democracy and Governance* 1, no. 2 (2013); K. O. Agutu, "The Impact of Ownership on Media Content: An Exploratory Case Study of Nation Media Group and Standard Newspaper Group; Kenya" (Thesis, University of the Witwatersrand); Beverly G. Hawk, *Africa's Media Image* (London: Praeger, 1992).

20 Petra Guatsi and Zdenka Mansfeldova, "Perception of Terrorism and Security and the Role of Media," *Paper prepared for the 7th ECPR General Conference*, Bordeaux, France, 4–7 September, 2013, 1.

21 Abraham K. Kisang, "Reporting Terrorism Among Kenyan Media: Should Journalists be Cautious," *Journal of Media and Communication Studies* 6, no. 5 (2014): 78–84.

22 Fredrik Ogenga, "Is Peace Journalism Possible in the War Against Terror in Somalia?"; Fredrik Ogenga, "From Al-Qaeda to Al-Shabaab: The Global and Local Implications of Terror in Kenya and East Africa," *Africa Journal of Democracy and Governance* 2, no. 3–4 (2015).

23 Martha Crenshaw, "The Causes of Terrorism," *Comparative Politics* 13, no. 4 (1981): 379–399; Martha Crenshaw, "The Psychology of Terrorism," *Political Psychology* 21, no. 2 (2002): 405–418; Max Abrahms, "What Terrorists Really Want: Terrorist Motives and Counter Terrorism Strategy," *International Security* 132, no. 4 (2008): 78–105; Albert Bergesen and Omar Lizardo, "International Terrorism and the World System," *Sociology Theory* 11, no. 1 (2004): 38–52; Todd Sandler, "New Frontiers in Terrorism Research: An Introduction," *Journal of Peace Research* 148, no. 3 (2011): 279–286.

24 Max Abrahms, "What Terrorists Really Want."

25 Daya Thussu, "How Media Manipulates Truth About Terrorism," *Economic and Political Weekly* 32, no. 6 (1997): 264–267; Laura K. Donohue, "Mediating Terror," *International Studies Review* 5, no. 2 (2003): 232–237.

26 (Frey, 1988; Hoffman, 1998; Wilkinson, 2000; Frey 2004).

27 Guatsi and Mansfeldova, "Perception of Terrorism and Security and the Role of Media".

28 Guatsi and Mansfeldova, "Perception of Terrorism and Security and the Role of Media," 2.

29 Guatsi and Mansfeldova, "Perception of Terrorism and Security and the Role of Media".

30 Dominic Rohner and Bruno Frey, "Blood and Ink! The Common Interest Game Between Terrorists and the Media," *Public Choice* 133, no. 1 (2007): 129–145.

31 Anne Rathbone and Charles K. Rowley, "Terrorism," *Public Choice* 112, nos. 3–4 (2002): 215–224; Sandler, "New Frontiers in Terrorism Research"; Rohner and Frey, "Blood and Ink!"; Beth Elise Whitaker, "Exporting the

Patriotic Act? Democracy and the War on Terror in the Third World," *Third World Quarterly* 28, no. 5 (2007): 1017–1032; Todd Sandler and KhrsravGaibulloe, "The Adverse Effects of Transnational and Domestic Terrorism on Growth in Africa," *Journal of Peace Research* 48, no. 3 (2011): 355–371; Michelle Slone, "Responses to Media Coverage of Terrorism," *Journal of Conflict Resolution* 44, no. 4 (2000): 508–522.

32 Wanjiru Kamau, "Kenya and the War on Terrorism," *Review of African Political Economy* 33, no. 107 (2006): 133–141; Jeremy Presdtholt, "Kenya, the United States, and Counterterrorism," *African Today* 57, no. 4 (2011): 2–27.

33 Fredirck Ogenga, "Is Peace Journalism Possible in the War Against Terror in Somalia?".

5 Re-situating local mass media

A tool for peacebuilding among the Abakuria in Kenya

John Oluoch

Conflict as questioning, dialogue, struggle, or debate is universal and found within families, communities, and nations. The number of major conflicts around the world today is considerable – Kenya is not an exception. Most conflicts are characterized by violence; many are still unresolved and have created deadlocks in international, regional, and local relations. The understanding of the root causes of conflicts and their management has increasingly become very dynamic. However, it is the conflicts that are linked to ethnicity that are more significant, despite attracting less attention worldwide.

More often than not, the focus has been on inter-ethnic conflicts in Africa at the expense of intra-ethnic conflict. Conflict can emerge among members of the same ethnic group as a result of scarce natural resources, as is the case among the Abakuria of Kenya. Several intra-ethnic conflicts of varying scale and intensity have occurred this century. Many of those involved in intra-ethnic conflicts are driven by grievances against perceived socioeconomic and political exclusion. Researchers have identified intra-ethnic conflict as having its origin in a contest for political power and scarce resources rather than diverging cultural affiliations involving ethnic markers.[1]

According to A. K. Sikuku, there have been multiple cases of intra-ethnic clashes in Kenya, the major one being the conflict among Sabaots residing in and around the Mount Elgon region, which has pit the Sabaot Land Defence Force of the Soy clan against the Moorland Forces of the Mosop clan, resulting in massive loss of lives and destruction of property.[2]

The Abakuria conflict

No intra-ethnic conflict in Kenya has been so profound yet unnoticed as the one among the Abakuria community.[3] This ethnic group occupies the southwestern tip of Kenya along the Kenya–Tanzania border, falling largely in Migori County. The county is multi-ethnic, home also to Luos, Luhyas, and some pockets of Somalis.[4] The Kuria community is made up of four clans: the Bakira, the Bagumbe, the Banyabasi, and the Bairege. All four clans speak exactly the same tongue (with minor differences) and are similar in most respects.[5] The Abakuria are both pastoralists and agriculturalists, although in recent years they have become predominantly agriculturalist.

Like many other instances of intra-ethnic conflict in Kenya, this one is based on clan differences and has led to extensive destruction and death without regard to gender and age. The construction of clan identity in the Abakuria ethnic community has increasingly been used as the basis for the allocation of political offices. Scholars have argued that the Abakuria conflict has become perpetual.[6] The conflict between the clans escalated to its most intense between 1986 and 1996. More recently, between July and September 2009, clashes between the two main clans – Nyabasi and Bwirege – resulted in the displacement of more than 20,000 people and left up to 200 people dead and much property destroyed.

The clashes in Kuria East District that began in 2009 were rooted in disagreements caused by cattle rustling, political differences over the division of the former Kuria District, and disputes over the location of the current headquarters in Kegonga Division – where the Nyabasi clan resides. The Bwirege clan demanded that the district headquarters be located in Ntimaru Division while the Nyabasi clan wanted the headquarters to remain in Kegonga. Due to these divergences of opinion, the clans viewed themselves as being involved in direct competition. In 2009 alone, more than 100 houses were burned down, more than 1,500 animals were driven away, crops in the fields were destroyed, granaries were burned down, and more than 180 deaths were recorded, with over 1,500 families becoming internally displaced. Others were forced to camp out in various market centers, churches, police stations, and with their relatives in what they called "safe homes." Publicly voiced opinions reportedly incited divisions between the two clans.[7] Historically, the Nyabasi and Bwirege clans have clashed over their competition for scarce resources, such as farmland, livestock, and grazing lands. In addition, the conflict cycle patterns in Kuria East District have involved cattle raids, which can be partially attributed to cultural practices relating to the use of cattle for paying a dowry for marriage following the initiation rites of passage.

The conflict has led to significant problems, such as youth from both clans being forced to suspend schooling or drop out altogether to seek safety among their respective clans during periods of conflict, which seriously interrupts their learning. Schools situated along the border between the clans are forced to close down, if they are not destroyed altogether. Inter-clan marriages have also suffered as women from the opposing clans have been forced to flee to their respective homes as they are threatened with death, with some being killed in the process of attempting to flee. This is often followed by the emergence of armed militias among the clans in the name of self-defense, which leads to more violence and destruction. A solution to these problems is therefore an urgent necessity. To foster long-lasting peace, these conflicts among the Abakuria need to be resolved decisively and the media, through peace journalism, should lead such efforts.

Community-based or ethnic-oriented mass media offers content that commercial and public outlets cannot provide and can therefore serve remote geographic communities and their interests. The content of these broadcasts is largely popular and relevant to a specific and/ or local audience but may often be overlooked by commercial or mass media broadcasters.[8] Indigenous language mass media serves listeners by offering a wider variety of local content that is not necessarily provided by the larger commercial media companies that have to place more emphasis on profit and audience. In exploring the importance of sharing information locally and opening up wider information networks, rural mass media is effective in improving the sharing of vital information within remote rural communities. Mass media in this regard provides a set of participatory communication techniques that support community dialogue by using local languages to communicate directly with community members, including youth and women, regarding issues of importance to that specific community.

Broadcast media in Kenya

The use of mass broadcast media in Kenya started with the launch of the Kenya Broadcasting Corporation (KBC) radio and TV channels in Nairobi which broadcast to the entire nation.[9] The programs were aired in English, Kiswahili, Hindu, and eleven other local languages. By 1964, KBC had established three national broadcasting services and two regional stations in Mombasa and Kisumu. It was not until 1953 when the first broadcasting service was created for Africans – appropriately named African Broadcasting Services. It carried programs in Kiswahili, Dholuo, Kikuyu, Kalenjin, Kiluhya, Kikamba, and Arabic. It is worth noting that the Kuria language was not among those that found their way onto the airwaves during this period.

Following the liberalization of the airwaves in Kenya from 2003, major media houses started radio stations with a view to targeting specific demographic groups by playing certain musical genres and speaking various local languages. The Voice of Kenya, the only mass media broadcaster in the country by then, went on to establish 19 radio stations that were broadcast in different parts of the country. The state agency offered three domestic services: the national service in Kiswahili, the general service in English, and vernacular service in 14 local languages. The vernacular/indigenous language services offered 184 hours every week for each language. Among the local languages which had been given a slot by the national broadcaster KBC, Kikuria only had two hours of airtime from 11 a.m. to 1 p.m. These broadcasts were also only allowed from Monday to Friday, excluding weekends when the majority of listeners were at home and more likely to listen to their radios. It should also be noted that the hours allocated for Kikuria broadcasts are not prime, invariably resulting in very low listenership and, therefore, a missed opportunity to use local radio among the Kuria for peacebuilding.

Local media and violence in Kenya

The indigenous language mass media broadcasting landscape in Kenya has changed over the last decade under the management of the Communication Authority of Kenya, which licenses stations that broadcast in vernacular languages. Kameme FM, which broadcasts in the Kikuyu language, was the first purely vernacular station to be set up in 2000, eventually leading to a proliferation of commercial, state-run, and community-based vernacular stations. Native language radio stations, in particular, have exploded, with the latest data showing that they have increased tenfold over the last decade from 10 in 1999 to more than 120 in 2015. In total, there are more than 100 active FM radio stations in Kenya, some of which are Kass FM and Chamgei FM (Kalenjin); Coro FM, Kameme FM, and Inooro FM (Kikuyu); Ramogi FM, Radio Lake Victoria, Lolwe FM, and Radio Mayienga (Luo); Mulembe FM and Sulwe FM (Luhya); Musyi FM (Kamba); and Egesa FM (Kisii). As stated earlier, none of the stations broadcast in the Abakuria language.

Local broadcasting is instrumental in helping developing countries like Kenya combat economic, political, educational, health, and social-cultural challenges. Ethnic tensions, human rights abuses, and corruption in government can be addressed through vernacular radio programs. Low literacy levels in rural areas and health issues, such as infant mortality, maternal deaths, and communicable diseases, are best addressed through tailor-made radio programs broadcast in various vernacular languages through the radio – since radio is cheap and accessible through ordinary internet-enabled cell phones. Considering that cell phone penetration in rural Kenya is high, indigenous language radio that speaks to the local context has the potential to work wonders in conflict resolution due to the large audience reach.

The media, whether traditional (e.g., radio, television and newspapers) or contemporary (21st-century) media (e.g., internet and mobile telephones), can be a potent tool either for fomenting and escalating conflict or for ameliorating and resolving it. This idea is fortified by the example of the Rwandan genocide of 1994 where a private radio establishment, Radio Télévision Libre des Mille Collines, was used to rally one ethnic group to commit massacres and try to wipe out another group. The use of mass media to mitigate inter-ethnic tensions during the Kenyan postelection violence in late 2007 and early 2008 is a well-documented example of media use for conflict de-escalation and resolution.

Kenya's vibrant media has been accused of having been ill prepared for the 2007–08 postelection violence that rocked the country following the disputed presidential results of the 2007 general election. The Kenyan media has been variously accused of failing to communicate the election results and news about the subsequent violence without partisan flavor. Various media houses, especially local language radio stations, stood accused of stirring tensions by taking sides and providing politicians with avenues to disseminate hate speech. A radio journalist with one of the local radio stations in Kenya, Joshua Arap Sang, was indicted by the International Criminal Court (ICC) on charges of crimes against humanity. The ICC prosecutor alleged that Sang used his Kalenjin-language radio program during the postelection violence to incite one community against another.

During the 2013 general elections, some members of the Kenyan media played a crucial role in informing, educating, and providing space for dialogue and a spirit of peace, tranquility, and restraint from acts of violence. These media stations practiced a considerably high degree of self-censorship by adopting the prevailing peace discourse. They were accused of failing to fulfill their role as a watchdog and neglecting to act in the best interest of the public. The media was accused of imposing self-censorship before, during, and immediately after the 2013 elections with respect to broadcasting sensitive issues and topics that might incite or ignite violence. The media was said to be highly cautious, restrained, and invariably hesitant. Critics said they lacked courage and objectivity and did not delve deep enough into the issues as they should have done.

Critics have also argued that the prevailing peace discourse at the time of the election was the fundamental reason why the media resorted to self-censorship. The general feeling was that the 2007–08 violence was to be avoided in 2013 at all costs. The barrage of peace messages from both the government and civil society via the mass media urged Kenyans to maintain peace and accept the results of the election whichever way they went. The media was keen to salvage its image after accepting culpability for the violence that took place in 2007–08 and was determined not to be blamed for another round of violence.

It is worth observing, however, that researchers and practitioners have tended to give more attention to the negative role of media in conflicts rather than its ameliorating effect. Etyan Giboa has observed that

> [d]espite the critical significance of the roles played by media in conflict and conflict resolution, this area has been relatively neglected by both scholars and practitioners. Most existing studies focus on the often negative contributions of the media to the escalation and violence phases of conflict. Very few studies deal with the actual or potential media contributions to conflict resolution and reconciliation.[10]

A well-grounded approach to the exposition of the actual and potential benefits of media in conflict resolution and reconciliation lies in understanding the broad range of media effects. There are limitations inherent in focusing on the media as prime movers or cause of particular events. Elizabeth Perse has suggested that the reason why many studies on media effects have produced minimal evidence of such effect could be that "media effects might be obscured by methodological imprecision, theoretical forces, and many personal, social, and situational constraints." To Perse, "the probe for media effects demands continued efforts, refined theories and methods, and the integration of a wide range of intervening variables into research designs."[11] It is therefore arguable that there is a need for more investigation of media effects using refined approaches and based on sound theory to establish the actual effects of the media on society rather than (like the proverbial desert ostrich) avoid confronting the problem and assuming that media effects do not exist in any significant way. It is in this regard that this chapter interrogates the potency of local radio in resolving a long-lasting intra-ethnic conflict among the Abakuria people of south-western Kenya.

Local media potential for peacebuilding in Kenya

A majority of Kenya's rural population depends on the radio as the most readily available source of important information and news. The information and broadcasting industry has exponentially developed and has great potential to provide rural populations with many benefits, including access to information and educational materials in different languages and forms. Broadcasting in indigenous languages has provided opportunities to rural populations who are more proficient in their mother tongue than in Kiswahili and English, the languages largely used on major radio stations. This model of local broadcasting targets rural audiences who are mostly concentrated in particular regions and speak a given language. This makes rural areas the focal points for vernacular broadcasting, which means that the radio broadcasts are regional and ethnic but not national.

Rural audiences are not highly regarded by traditional media (who need to sell airtime to advertisers) because of their low purchasing power and higher poverty rates. Therefore, the uptake of television and traditional media is still low and slow in rural areas compared to urban areas. The role played by local radio in influencing development in these rural areas cannot be overstated. It addresses a large section of the rural population due to their familiarity with the language and content of its broadcasts. The centrality of the rural population to government policy formulation and activities of nongovernmental organizations that are concerned with improving the living conditions and standards of the underprivileged communities can become spin-offs from the creative use of local broadcasting.

Curiously, the real scale and magnitude of the Abakuria conflict do not get prominent coverage in the mainstream national media. What is normally reported is cattle theft among the Abakuria, with hardly any indication about the magnitude or impact of the so-called cattle theft. It is therefore not clear how the mass media has assisted in the resolution of the intra-ethnic conflicts in Abakuria. It is also worth examining whether cattle theft alone would qualify as intra-ethnic conflict or simply theft, which would demand a different response mechanism. However, if cattle theft escalates in number and transforms into large-scale cattle rustling by armed nonstate actors, then intra-ethnic conflict is alive and kicking. In the latter, local radio could play a key role in conflict resolution.

This chapter brings to the fore two important arguments: first, intra-ethnic conflict is an important phenomenon in its own right, leading to thousands of deaths and population displacements throughout the world. Second, conflict within homogeneous groups is intimately connected to conflict between heterogeneous groups. A complete understanding of ethnic conflict processes will be impossible without a better grasp of the forces responsible for generating intra-ethnic cohesion and fragmentation. Finally, the study of intra-ethnic conflict provides a useful perspective on the nature of group identities, highlighting the mutable characters of group boundaries and the need for response theories that transcend assumptions of fixed cleavages.

This chapter argues for a "ready to go" prescription for the use of local broadcast media in resolving or ameliorating a long-standing ethnic conflict in Kenya. Ethnic harmony is priceless as it forms the very foundation on which other development projects – in education, health, and infrastructure – are based. No society can develop amid incessant violent conflict, as witnessed among the Abakuria. A close analysis reveals that rural-based media is a strategic communication initiative appropriate for a specific audience in a specific manner – whether written, printed, broadcast, or spoken – and it is intended to reach and have an impact on a large and homogenous audience in a manner that can be predetermined. This includes television, radio, advertising, movies, the internet, newspapers, magazines, and so forth.

If this is the case, it therefore means that mass media delivered via indigenous languages is a significant factor in the culture of those who share in that language, particularly in terms of their social interactions and collective aspirations as a people. Sociologists refer to this as a mediated culture, where media continuously reflects and re-creates the culture. Communities and individuals are constantly bombarded with mass media messages that promote not only products but also moods, attitudes, beliefs, behavior, and a sense of what is and is not important to them as a people. In the same vein, the message of peace can be broadcast with similar energy for peacebuilding.

The role of media in the resolution of intra-ethnic violence

In order to objectively understand the nature and the role of media in peace and conflict management, it is important to understand the various ways through which local media influences conflict and conflict management. The growing recognition of the crucial role the media can play in helping provoke conflict has led many to examine how the media can play a constructive role in resolving conflict. One limitation of the discussion about peace journalism is that it speaks to only part of the reality of the modern media where the media is an actor in its own right. Part of the problem with the debate about "peace journalism" is confusion about the different roles of the media. The media is a place in which journalists convey ideas, information, and stories to the listener, viewer, or reader – in this way they project a version of reality. It is sometimes said that the journalist acts as a vehicle that conveys the different views, outlooks, and perspectives in society. In this capacity, there is fierce resistance to any attempt to encroach on the independence of journalists carrying out this function or any attempt to impose an ideological purpose on them, however worthy. The media understood in this way is a structure that reflects the debates of society.

However, in addition to the representation of the groups they are reporting on – in this case, parties to a conflict – journalists also present their own views and interests. In this respect, the media itself becomes an actor in the conflict, for example, when it takes an editorial position or focuses on certain issues or aspects of the conflict to the exclusion of others. The idea that the journalist sits outside of the events they are covering, whatever their perspective on "peace journalism," could be misleading. The members of the media, in this sense, are themselves actors and agents in the conflict and their behavior will inevitably have an effect on the way the conflict develops.

To use more abstract terms, the media constitutes a space in which the conflicts of a society can be articulated and its members are inevitably themselves actors in that conflict. Moreover, the combatants in a conflict will usually relate to each other either on the battlefield or in the way they are represented in the media (the latter, as is evident in many recent conflicts, may often be more important to them than the battlefield). To use sociological terms, the media is both a structure and an agency. The idea that it can be a simple instrument of any point of view – state or nonstate – could be profoundly misleading, and a policy toward the media in the context of conflict has to take into account the sense in which they play both of these interweaving roles.

Policymakers need to focus on the media's role in (re)constituting the public sphere: how it can be fostered and nurtured in such a way as to allow nonviolent resolution of conflict. The "public sphere" refers to the range of communication outlets and media which enable a society to view the representations of itself. To function properly, a public sphere must have free-flowing access to information and enable the views of ordinary citizens to be heard. It should not be assumed that conflict itself is wrong or can be avoided in any society. The clash of interests, needs, and desires balanced against the allocation of scarce resources means that conflict is inevitable in any given society. Where the media can play a vital role in allowing a peace process to develop is by enabling the underlying conflicts in a society to be expressed and argued in a nonviolent manner. This requires the creation of a suitable media space in which this can happen.

A number of organizations have begun considering how to create situations in conflict and postconflict environments that allow the media to play a constructive role in tackling conflict. It has been increasingly recognized that an effective media is essential to preventing violent conflict from breaking out and an important element in its resolution should it break out. There is an increasing number of attempts to produce a more comprehensive and coherent policy approach to this problem.

On October 5–6, 2003, International Media Support convened a roundtable in Copenhagen to examine conflict reporting. It acknowledged that there was no consensus on the best approach to conflict reporting among media professionals. The roundtable considered how conflict reporting impacted on war and how such reporting could be improved. The focus was on recent conflicts, and participants sought to explore the distinction between peace journalism and conflict sensitive journalism through analyzing specific interventions on conflict reporting.

Some participants suggested that the best approach might be to examine what the professional responsibilities of journalists should be in a conflict arena. This would include avoiding portraying conflicts as a zero-sum game contested by two combatants but, rather, disaggregating the various interests that clash. It also would involve seeking to humanize both parties – making it clear that sometimes (although not always) there are no simple villains and victims.

In recent years, there has been a profusion of projects and initiatives designed to support and promote peace journalism of one kind or another. Most focus on professional training initiatives to promote better coverage of issues related to diverse identities or differences and encourage reports on peace initiatives. The Canadian-based Institute for Media Policy and Civil Society suggests five kinds of peace interventions, including training, promoting positive images, and providing fictional storylines that have a positive peace message. Some of these approaches are little more than applying the best techniques of professional journalism to conflict reporting. However, the very term *peace journalism* causes many journalists real concern. They argue that society needs information and the exchange of ideas and opinions in the public sphere. The media, they say, must be free to play its role in fulfilling that obligation. Arguing that the media promotes peace suggests to those in the media the sense of an ideologically committed journalism.

Some media organizations have argued that the very practice of good professional journalism is itself a form of conflict resolution. In conflict-affected settings, the provision of reliable information is crucial and is often difficult to provide. The provision of accurate information about a conflict is therefore a priority for all agencies and developing and maintaining a culture of professional journalism is important.

As has been noted, the media can be a crucial weapon in stoking and fanning conflicts and wars. On the other hand, the media can be a constructive tool in helping resolve conflicts and bringing about peace. The quest for the media to be involved in conflict resolution has developed tension between the need for the media to remain objective without taking sides and the need to be passionate about the cause of peace. Many have called on the media to assume the mantle of championing the cause of peace by delving into the underlying causes of conflicts. Taking such a path will lead to better analyses of the objectives of all the actors in a conflict and finding ways to resolve the conflict. Whereas conflict is an extreme form of communication, the media can play a vital role in allowing a peace process to develop and thereafter flourish by enabling underlying conflicts to be expressed and argued in a nonviolent manner.

To achieve this requires the creation of a suitable media space within society through the establishment of an appropriate media framework and practices landscape. In light of the proliferation of mass media technology, a responsive media policy is needed. This will allow the media to play a constructive role in tackling conflict without losing its primary role. Any attempt to prevent violent conflict from breaking out requires the presence of an effective and responsive media that is within reach of community members. This is where the importance of local radio stations in rural communities, as in the case of the Abakuria, becomes clear.

Notes

1 Stuart J. Kaufman, *Modern Hatreds: The Symbolic Politics of Ethnic War* (Ithaca: Cornell University Press, 2001).
2 Paul Abuso Sikuku, "The Land Question and Intra-Ethnic Conflict in Squatter Enclaves of Mt. Elgon Region, Western Kenya" (Unpublished Thesis, Masinde Muliro University-CDMHA, 2011).

3 David Mwangi Kungu, Risper Omari, and Stanley Kipsang, "A Journey into the Indigenous Conflict Management Mechanisms among the Abakuria Community, Kenya: 'The Beauty and the Beast'," *European Scientific Journal* 11, no. 16 (2015): 202–217.

4 Paul Asaka Abuso, *A Traditional History of the Abakuria c. AD 1400–1914* (Nairobi: Kenya Literature Bureau, 1980).

5 Abuso, *A Traditional History of the Abakuria*.

6 Kungu, Omari, and Kipsang, "A Journey into the Indigenous Conflict Management Mechanisms Among the Abakuria Community, Kenya".

7 Kungu, Omari, and Kipsang, "A Journey into the Indigenous Conflict Management Mechanisms Among the Abakuria Community, Kenya".

8 Theodor Adorno and Max Horkheimer, *The Dialectic of Enlightenment*, eds. Gunzclin Schmid Noerrand, trans. Edmund Jephcott (Stanford: Stanford University Press, 2012).

9 Edwin Okoth, "The Emergence and Growth of Vernacular Radio in Kenya: A Case Study of Radio Having a Positive Economic Impact," *Reuters Institute Fellowship Paper*, University of Oxford, 2015.

10 Eytan Gilboa, "Media and Conflict Resolution: A Framework for Analysis," *Maruette. Literature Review* 93, no. 1 (2009): 88.

11 Elizabeth M. Perse, *Media Effects and Society* (Mahwah: Lawrence Erlbaum Associates, 2001), 14.

6 Media and peace in Kenya

Do journalists need different skills?

Victor Bwire

Since the 2017 general election in Kenya and the ensuing postelection violence, the role of the media in peacebuilding has come under scrutiny. Elections in Kenya have often been marred by political, ethnic, and other forms of conflict before and after the voting process. Over the past three decades the country has experienced multiple conflicts linked to politically motivated violence. The ways that the Kenyan media have often reported on such incidents of political violence have also heightened tensions during such periods.[1]

High stakes in general elections

Given the high stakes in the 2017 general election, the atmosphere of general insecurity (heightened by the threat of terrorist attacks), and polarization along political and ethnic lines, the media is seen as a key player in the country's peacebuilding efforts. Several interventions aimed at educating journalists and members of the public on the need for national cohesion and peaceful coexistence ahead of the 2017 general elections have been implemented.

The decision to place media at the core of peacebuilding in Kenya was premised on case studies, including the tragedy of the Rwandan genocide of 1994, the postelection violence of 2007–08 in Kenya, and the spate of terror-related attacks. A commission of inquiry concluded that the media was as much to blame for the mayhem as the political class – not in initiating the violence but by amplifying the messages of hate mainly through the local radio stations.[2]

Media law and regulation

Media support groups in Kenya are aware of the limitations journalists face. Several measures were put in place ahead of the 2017 general election to strengthen existing laws regulating media coverage of political and ethnic violence and terrorism. These include the Prevention of Terrorism Act and the National Intelligence Service Act in 2012, the Proceeds of Crime and Anti-Money Laundering Act in 2009, and the Prevention of Organized Crime Act in 2010. In addition, a number of administrative pronouncements and policy statements have been made by the authorities targeted at the media, clearly indicating that the media must change the way it covers matters of national security.

The constitution provides for the right to information for the media and other Kenyans, particularly in matters of national importance, as the media has a responsibility to inform the public on matters that affect their lives.[3] The information flow from the policymakers and the government has been problematic for members of the media, sometimes frustrating their work. The increased control of media coverage of terrorism, including the harassment of the media in the war on terrorism and violent extremism, is usually justified by the government on grounds of national security. In some cases, the government has expressed concern about poor-quality work and a lack of ethics on the part of some journalists whose reports end up supporting terrorism by giving publicity to acts of terrorism, thereby helping to spread fear and anxiety among members of the public.

A major challenge facing journalists covering terrorism and security-related events is increased conflict with Kenya's security institutions. Journalists have experienced intimidation, physical attacks, trauma, loss of equipment, and some have also been co-opted by the government. Counterterrorism experts argue that the emergence of the information revolution has led to the development of new and expansive communication technologies with instant worldwide reach that fuels the phenomenon of "mega-terrorism." The questions then are, How do we balance national security with the public's right to information? and Should we allow everyone – terrorists included – to compete in the marketplace of ideas and hope the public will make the right choices?

There is a need to strengthen the professionalism underpinning media coverage of elections, terrorism, violent extremism, and counterterrorism as an important step toward enhancing mutual understanding between the media and security institutions. Journalists must be aware of the consequences their reporting may have on society despite the pressures of accuracy, deadlines, objectivity, and even patriotism. They must also ensure that every story is based on facts rather than emotions. There are several policies and laws in Kenya that exist to guide the practice of journalism; some of the most important include the following:

- Article 33 of the constitution provides for freedom of expression but adds a rider that the right to freedom of expression does not extend to propaganda for war, incitement to violence, or hate speech – which includes advocacy of hatred that constitutes ethnic incitement, vilification of others, incitement to cause harm, or speech based on any type of discrimination specified or contemplated in Article 27.[4]
- The Media Council Act 2013, through the Code of Ethics for the practice of journalism in Kenya, has specific provisions that require journalists to guard against stories that could be seen to incite people to violence, including Article 23, which concerns acts of violence, provides that the media shall avoid presenting acts of violence, armed robberies, banditry, and terrorist activities in a manner that glorifies such antisocial conduct. Newspapers shall not allow their columns to be used for writings which tend to encourage or glorify social evils, warlike activities, and ethnic, racial, or religious hostilities.[5]
- Article 4 on integrity provides that journalists shall present news with integrity and common decency, avoiding real or perceived conflicts of interest and respecting the dignity and intelligence of the audience as well as the subjects of news.[6]
- Article 12 – covering ethnic, religious, and sectarian conflict – requires that news, views, or comments on ethnic, religious, or sectarian disputes shall be published or broadcast after proper verification of facts and presented with due caution and restraint in a manner that is conducive to the creation of an atmosphere congenial to national harmony, unity, and peace.[7]
- Article 15 on intrusion into grief and shock provides that in cases involving personal grief or shock, inquiries shall be made with sensitivity and discretion.[8]
- On the use of pictures and names, Article 21 provides that as a general rule the media shall apply caution in the use of pictures and names and shall avoid publication when there is a possibility of harming the persons concerned. The manipulation of pictures in a manner that distorts reality and accuracy of news shall be avoided. Pictures of grief, disaster, those that embarrass, and those that promote sexism shall be discouraged.[9]
- Article 25 on hate speech provides that quoting persons making derogatory remarks based on ethnicity, race, creed, color, and sex shall not be allowed.[10]
- The Kenya Information and Communications Act 2013 has specific rules and regulations for the media through the "Programming

Code" for free-to-air television and radio broadcasters. The guide-lines are as follows:

a   The coverage of crimes in progress or crisis situations shall not put lives in greater danger than is already inherent in the situation.

b   Coverage should avoid inflicting undue shock and pain to families and loved ones of victims of crimes, crisis situations, disasters, accidents, and other tragedies.

c   The identity of victims of crimes or crisis situations in progress shall not be announced until the situation has been resolved or their names have been released by the authorities.

d   Coverage of crime or crisis situations shall not provide vital information or offer comfort or support to the perpetrators.[11]

- Section 66 of the Kenyan Penal Code provides that any person who publishes any false statement, rumor, or report that is likely to cause fear and alarm to the public or to disturb the public peace is guilty of a misdemeanor. However, the publisher can be absolved if prior to publication, it took measures to verify the accuracy of the statement, rumor, or report as to lead them to reasonably believe that it was true.[12]

- Section 52 on the "power to prohibit publications" empowers the government to, on "reasonable grounds," prohibit the importation of any publication or declare any publication to be a prohibited in the interests of public order, health or morals, and the security of Kenya.[13]

- Section 67, relating to the Defamation Act, makes it an offense for anyone to publish anything that threatens to degrade any foreign dignitary "with the intent to disturb peace and friendship" between Kenya and the country to which the dignitary belongs.[14]

- The Official Secrets Act provides that any person who "obtains, collects, records, publishes or communicates in whatever manner to any other person" any "information which is calculated to be or might be or is intended to be directly or indirectly useful to a foreign power or disaffected person" commits an offense. "Any person who takes a photograph of a prohibited place or who takes a photograph in a prohibited place, without having first obtained the authority of the officer in charge of the prohibited place, shall be guilty of an offence."[15] A person found guilty can be jailed for up to five years.

- Section 9A of the Prevention of Terrorism Act of 2012 provides that anyone who "advocates, promotes, advises, or facilitates" the

commission of a terrorist act or any act preparatory to a terrorist act is liable to imprisonment for a term not exceeding twenty
years. Section 12D on radicalization criminalizes anyone who
"adopts or promotes an extreme belief system for the purpose of
facilitating ideologically based violence to advance political, religious or social change." This offense is punishable by a maximum
of 30 years.[16]

The Media Council of Kenya captured the importance of sensitive
news coverage in times of conflict in a 2016 publication called *The
Anatomy of Conflict: A Conflict Analysis Handbook for Journalists;
Towards Conflict Sensitive Reporting.* The book features emerging
discourses on how the media is expected to carefully balance media
freedom and responsible reporting of sensitive national issues as out-
lined in the Code of Conduct for the Practice of Journalism and the
constitution. Apart from guaranteeing the freedom of expression, the
constitution also calls on practitioners to understand that the right to
freedom of expression does not extend to propaganda for war, incitement to violence, hate speech, or advocacy of hatred that constitutes
ethnic incitement, vilification of others, or incitement to cause harm.

Creating awareness

The media can help people to identify and understand the dimensions
and root causes of a conflict. Journalists can raise awareness about
what needs to happen in order for a conflict to be effectively resolved.
By anticipating how a conflict might develop, journalists can ask
questions that raise awareness about the potentially harmful effects
of allowing a conflict to escalate. By identifying the ways in which
parties are approaching conflicts, journalists can pose questions that
highlight the strengths and weaknesses of the competitive and collab-
orative approaches that parties adopt in pursuing the conflict.

The Kenyan media has for the last decade played a crucial role in
advancing democratic governance, reforms, and accountability in the
country. It continues to play a central part in the ongoing political,
legal, and constitutional reforms in the country. It is now evident,
therefore, that a strong, independent, and professional media can
make a positive contribution to national cohesion and peacebuilding
by presenting diverse opinions and ideas on issues of public interest
that inform people in their choice of leaders both at the national and
county government levels. Thus, improving professionalism and effec-
tiveness of media practitioners and strengthening the existing media

landscape are crucial preelection preparatory processes and appropriate responses to terrorism.

The 2007 postelection violence saw many people accusing the media of irresponsible reporting that led to electoral violence. The tendency to focus on side issues instead of sharing information that would empower, educate, and sensitize the public was one of the shortcomings of media coverage at the time. One of the lessons learned was the need for the media to pay greater attention to the task of creating a public sphere: the "space" within which ideas, opinions, and views freely circulate. It is imperative that the media is prepared to take this central role.

Training journalists

Based on the foregoing, many experts have argued that media practitioners, if properly trained and equipped, can play a critical role in helping communities understand historical injustices and how to address them, learn about the laws that exist to address conflicts, and promote peaceful coexistence.

As Howard Ross's maintains in his handbook, *My Tribe Is Journalism*, it is very important that journalists are well trained and equipped with skills that enable them to analyze conflict professionally and report from an informed standpoint. It is not the business of professional journalists to seek to alter, lessen, or disrupt the course of a conflict. However, they have the duty to present accurate, objective, and impartial news about conflicts to their publics. While the constraints of time and space are limiting factors in news production, journalists must learn to package their stories without eliminating the essential elements they have learned through their analysis of conflict. It should be noted that

> [c]onflict exists in a relationship when parties believe their aspirations cannot be achieved at the same time. They also perceive a divergence in their values, needs or interests (latent). They therefore mobilize the power that is available to them in an effort to eliminate, neutralize, influence, or change each other. The sole desire being to protect or further their interests in the interaction (manifest conflict). From this definition, several things are evident in relations to the nature of conflict.[17]

Accordingly, accurate, objective, and reliable reporting on conflict by journalists is very important. It can assist in reducing tensions by bringing out facts, correcting misperceptions, and presenting realities which would otherwise be ignored by conflicting parties. Quality reporting on conflict helps avoid stereotypes and narrow views about the causes and process of conflict. The media can explore and provide information about opportunities for resolution and help the parties into a dialogue by accurately reporting on the issues. This can only happen if journalists have a good understanding of conflict situations. Journalists have the potential to contribute to conflict escalation, interfere with peace processes, derail negotiations, and misinform the public through inaccurate, insensitive, and sensational reporting. Conflict analysis helps to create a broader, deeper, and objective understanding of the conflict situation in a way that enhances quality reporting.[18]

Scholars like Gary Furlong argue that "conflict can be viewed through a cultural lens, communications lens, personality lens, structural lens, type of conflict lens, dynamics of conflict lens, and many more."[19] Professional requirements set by the Media Council of Kenya dictate that journalists must look at conflict holistically with the aim of objective, accurate, and reliable reporting. When journalists are equipped with such a wide understanding and approach, they are likely to "avoid repeating shallow, thoughtless rhetoric about the conflict to achieve sensationalism and targets for their media houses."[20] Journalism that is conflict-sensitive equips media practitioners with the capacity to recognize that their role is to serve audiences and not to serve as a megaphone for any actor in a propaganda war.

For preventive action, training in conflict-sensitive journalism should be aimed at building journalists' awareness about the potentially pivotal role they can play in mediating or exacerbating conflict. Such initiatives entail working with the media to find a means of reporting that balances between two disparate positions and emphasizes peace promotion. Similarly, the media promotes peace by serving as an information conduit between dissenting groups and voices, thus reducing prejudice and stereotypes. In targeting the political elite, media interventions promote peace by placing pressure to move toward a resolution.

The conflict-sensitive journalism training and media stakeholder engagements implemented by the Media Council of Kenya and other media support groups are aimed at building journalists' awareness of their role. The power of the media to influence policy and stimulate intervention, thereby changing the course of a conflict, has been dubbed the "CNN Effect." This effect creates a triangular relationship among media, government, and the public and underscores the role of journalists as enablers of peace in the society.

Notes

1 *The Anatomy of Conflict: A Conflict Analysis Handbook for Journalists; Towards Conflict Sensitive Reporting* (Nairobi: Media Council of Kenya, 2016), www.mediacouncil.or.ke/en/mck/images/Gallery/Monitoring/Anat omy-of-Conflict.pdf
2 *Commission of Inquiry into the Post-Election Violence (CIPEV) Final Report* (Nairobi: Government of Kenya, 2008), https://reliefweb.int/report/kenya/ kenya-commission-inquiry-post-election-violence-cipev-final-report
3 *Constitution of Kenya*, 2010.
4 Article 33, *Constitution of Kenya*; Article 27, *Constitution of Kenya*.
5 Media Council Act, No. 46 of 2013; Article 23, *Constitution of Kenya*.
6 Article 4, *Constitution of Kenya*.
7 Article 12, *Constitution of Kenya*.
8 Article 15, *Constitution of Kenya*.
9 Article 21, *Constitution of Kenya*.
10 Article 25, *Constitution of Kenya*.
11 Kenya Information and Communications (Amendment) Act, No. 41A of 2013.
12 Kenyan Penal Code, Section 66(1).
13 Kenyan Penal Code, Section 52(1).
14 Kenyan Penal Code, Section 67.
15 Official Secrets Act, No. 31 of 2016.
16 Prevention of Terrorism Act, No. 30 of 2012.
17 *Anatomy of Conflict*, 12.
18 *Anatomy of Conflict*.
19 Gary T. Furlong, "Conflict Analysis Models for Mediators and Other Practitioners," *Mediate.com*, October 2002, www.mediate.com/articles/ furlong1.cfm
20 *Anatomy of Conflict*, 4.

7 Toward a peace and human rights approach to journalism

In search of social justice in postconflict situations in Africa

Jacinta Mwende Maweu

Introduction

The main argument of this chapter is that the major impediment to a peace and human rights approach to journalism lies in the media's structural subordination to the interests of political and economic elites. Both peace journalism and human rights journalism are relatively new modes of socially responsible journalism aimed at contributing to the peaceful settlement of conflicts.[1] Jake Lynch and Annabel McGoldrick define peace journalism as "when editors and reporters make choices – of what stories to report and about how to report them – that create opportunities for society at large to consider and value non-violent responses to conflict."[2] Human rights journalism, on the other hand, is journalism "with a human face; one that cares for people, that prioritizes people over capitalistic interests and above all the one that shields the public from the manipulations of the political and economic elite."[3] A human rights approach to journalism is anchored on the premise that "all people matter" (*Ubuntu* or *Utu*), which is a moral commitment to overcome the practice of "othering" when reporting on contentious issues, especially during times of war and conflict.

Johan Galtung, one of the earliest proponents of peace journalism makes a distinction between "peace journalism" and "war journalism." He argues that peace journalism is a "journalism of attachment" to all actual and potential victims whereas war journalism attaches only to "our" side. War journalism, according to Galtung's peace journalism model, is "propaganda-orientated" whereas peace journalism is "truth-orientated." Galtung criticizes the media for generally following the "low road" in reporting conflict by chasing wars and focusing on the elites that run them, as well as "win–lose" outcomes.[4] Both peace journalism and human rights journalism, as alternative forms of journalism, emphasize not only reporting the acts of political, social, or cultural violence but also asking questions about the reasons behind these acts and how they can be prevented or managed to minimize suffering.[5]

A human rights approach to journalism holds that the media should highlight the indirect structural and cultural violence – abuses of economic and sociocultural rights – prevalent in most conflict situations.[6] Human rights are fundamental freedoms to which all people are entitled; they are about being treated with dignity and respect. They are especially important to vulnerable and less powerful people, such as children, women, and people living with disabilities, whose rights are most at risk of violation in times of war and conflict.

Mass media and the protection of human rights

Independent journalism and a free media are the bedrock of democratic consolidation and respect for human rights. During times of conflict, truth and justice are the first casualties, especially if the media have been co-opted by the powers that be to play a propaganda role on their behalf, masking the reality that the same elites are also the main perpetrators of human rights violations during such times. Attempts by the media to make the facts known to the public are often the first essential step in redressing human rights violations and holding those in power accountable. The media should work with public authorities, civil society, and the international community to ensure the protection and promotion of human rights.

By exposing violations of rights, the media can improve the climate for democratic debate and reduce corruption and acts of impunity, which are major sources of human rights violations in public life. At the same time, media sensitivity to the importance of human rights provides reliable sources of information through which citizens, human rights groups, private organizations, and public authorities can work together to promote development and eliminate abuse.

As the people's watchdogs, agenda setters, public informers/educators, and the fourth estate, the media plays an important role in the promotion and protection of human rights. They have a moral obligation to expose human rights violations and offer an arena for different voices to be heard in public discourse. The media has the power to highlight human rights issues and the moral obligation to monitor, investigate, and report all human rights violations against anyone regardless of their socioeconomic status. To ensure social justice for the poor, human rights and peace journalists must endeavor to deconstruct the underlying causes of, for instance, the political violence prevalent in many Africa societies today, as opposed to only reporting about outbreaks of violence. Some of these causes are ethnicity, poverty, youth unemployment, and denial of minority rights.

Media manipulated by consent?

Although the media wields a lot of power that can be harnessed to achieve the goals of a just peace and human rights protection, this power is often abused or misused to provide a conducive environment for violations of such rights. Although members of the media are not simply agents of the powerful, there is a vast body of scholarly literature that suggests that news media focuses on powerful people and institutions and generally reflects established interests.[7] The way the media uses language to represent different social and political groups and to describe what events and issues are newsworthy tends to establish the dominant ways the rest of us to talk about those groups and events.[8]

During times of conflict, there are many factors that impact the rights of people, such as the international and national legal frameworks for rights, the cultural context in which the journalist is reporting, the socioeconomic situation of the country or region, and the political situation – all of which journalists should strive to contextualize and deconstruct. Many people in our society do not know their rights. The media can help them better understand their own lives, thereby strengthening their ability to stand up for their rights. By increasing public understanding, journalists increase opportunities for friendly coexistence and reduce the likelihood of conflicts based on misunderstanding, rumor, and misinformation. For most people, information filtered through the media is their main source of knowledge of various issues: "if the media didn't say or show it, then it didn't happen."

The media does set the agenda for the public through the way it frames issues and determines what issues are considered important. By omitting certain events and issues from the day's agenda and overemphasizing of others, the media establishes a particular way for its audience to think about reality.[9] More often, the media aligns itself with political and economic elites and their propaganda, sometimes even state propaganda, especially in times of war. On many occasions, political elites sometimes double up as media owners and therefore limit media freedom especially when it comes to reporting on issues touching on their own interests. Peace and human rights journalism, unlike war journalism, assesses the often deliberate and systematic attempts by mainstream media to represent political and economic elites as "worthy victims" and ordinary citizens as "unworthy victims" in cases of political violence. Peace and human rights journalism is supported by framing theory because it critically examines how journalists choose what to report on and how they report what they choose.[10] Framing and agenda setting are critical in peace and human rights journalism because any meaningful debate about journalism must include some effort to set out the basis on which some forms of representation should be preferred to others.[11]

Case studies

In Kenya, there are many occasions on which the mainstream media has largely succeeded in making the public "forget" about critical post-conflict issues by either downplaying them in their coverage or ignoring them altogether. Examples of this are media coverage of the 2007–08 postelection violence, the subsequent cases at the International Criminal Court (ICC), the 2013 general election, and the just-concluded 2017 general election.

During the 2007–08 postelection violence, the media were accused of taking the "low road" of war reporting by taking explicit political stands, thus fueling the conflict. With regard to the coverage of the ICC cases, the media was accused of downplaying and ignoring the plight of the helpless internally displaced persons by presenting them as the "unworthy victims" while portraying the minority political elite who stood accused of crimes as the "worthy victims" of the conflict. Human rights journalism calls on the media to objectively and impartially represent all parties involved in human rights violation and not portray elite victims as more worthy of rights (mainly the political and economic elites) and nonelites as being less worthy.

In the coverage of the 2013 general election, the media was accused of going overboard in promoting "peace at all costs," what can loosely be described as "peaceocracy," at the expense of justice and democracy and in the name of "peace journalism." Media coverage of the 2017 election appeared to repeat the mistakes of 2013. Although there were numerous alleged electoral malpractices, the media tended to give a lot of prominence to announcements by official sources, especially the Independent Elections and Boundaries Commission (IEBC), the police, and President Uhuru Kenyatta. Within the framework of human rights and peace journalism, the mainstream media in Kenya can be faulted for not engaging in critical reporting that investigates and interrogates claims by officials to explain and offer context and perspective on the issues raised. Journalists and the media have a moral obligation to connect the dots for the public.

There was also a deliberate move by the media to enforce a blackout on reports of postelection killings – mostly in the opposition strongholds of Kisumu, Siaya, Homa Bay, and Nairobi – and the use of excessive force against protesters by the Kenya Police after IEBC officially declared Kenyatta the president-elect. Journalism that steers clear of controversial claims by legitimate actors in the name of peace contributes to injustice and proves counterproductive in the long run. This is because it not only undermines the integrity and credibility of journalism but also undercuts the strengthening of state institutions such as the IBEC.

There was also a subsequent crackdown on vocal civil society organizations, such as the Kenya Human Rights Commission and the Africa Center for Open Governance. Although the media did highlight such crackdowns, there was a deliberate and rather worrying attempt not to ask the hard questions regarding the government's motives behind the crackdown, especially with a looming election petition by the opposition. One would have expected questions as to whether these organizations were paying the price for their election-related activism or if the crackdown's timing was just a coincidence. These are legitimate questions that journalists ought to have asked but failed to.

Conclusion

Journalists and the media hold the power to determine what is newsworthy and to construct stories and select words in ways that influence people's understanding of issues. The media has the capacity to inform the public, to connect remote worlds, and to shape an individual's knowledge and understanding of the world we live in. Journalists and the media have a professional and moral obligation to increase public awareness, to educate the public on their rights, and, most important, to help monitor human rights.

Journalists should not only report events; they should also provide in-depth analysis to put issues into context. Through in-depth analysis and the bringing together of multiple perspectives, journalists create the potential for a more knowledgeable, well-rounded, and aware public. This increased awareness could lead to a stronger civil society and a more active population that can stand up for its civil, political, and socioeconomic rights, which are grossly violated during times of conflict. Good journalism grounded on a peace and human rights framework should not avoid the ugly facts. It should instead accurately report on what is going on, interrogate the claims, and report them in a manner that helps the reader, listener, or viewer understand what is happening. Such reporting would also help in holding perpetrators to account.

Notes

1 Thomas Hanitzsch, "Journalists as Peacekeeping Force? Peace Journalism and Mass Communication Theory," *Journalism Studies* 5, no. 4 (2004): 483–495; Ibrahim Seaga Shaw, *Human Rights Journalism: Advances in Reporting Distant Humanitarian Interventions* (London: Palgrave Macmillan, 2012).
2 Jake Lynch and Annabel McGoldrick, *Peace Journalism* (Stroud, UK: Hawthorn Press, 2005), 5.
3 Shaw, *Human Rights Journalism*, 35–36.
4 Johan Galtung, "High Road, Low Road: Charting the Course for Peace Journalism," *Track Two: Constructive Approaches to Community and Political Conflict* 7, no. 4 (1998).
5 Jake Lynch, "What's So Great About Peace Journalism?" *Global Media Journal: Mediterranean Edition* 1, no. 1 (2006): 74–87.
6 Shaw, *Human Rights Journalism*, xi.
7 David Croteau and William Hoynes, *Media/Society: Industries, Images, and Audiences* (London: Sage, 2003), 169.
8 Linda Thomas and Shân Wareing, *Language, Society and Power* (London: Routledge, 1999), 50.
9 Pieter J. Fourie, *Media Studies: Media History, Media and Society*, 2nd ed. (Cape Town: Juta Academic, 2007), 304.
10 Seow Ting Lee, "Peace Journalism: Principles and Structural Limitations in the News Coverage of Three Conflicts," *Mass Communication and Society* 13, no. 4 (2010): 364.
11 Jake Lynch, "Peace Journalism and Its Discontents," *Conflict & Communication Online* 6, no. 2 (2007): 2.

Afterword
East Africa peace journalism

Steven Youngblood

The peace journalism (PJ) theory was developed by Westerners, chiefly Dr. Johan Galtung, Dr. Jake Lynch, and Annabel McGoldrick. Even though PJ is a Western construct, the writers in this book nonetheless believe PJ's principles are clearly applicable, perhaps with some modifications, in East Africa.

Kenyan academic Fredrick Ogenga writes, "Peace journalism brings together certain elements that are essential to promoting peace in East African countries. The enabling elements of this form of journalism include sensitivity, agility, caution, factual information, and self-reflectivity in relation to what media practitioners put into the content of news reports and editorials" (p. 39).

In addition to these "enabling" PJ elements listed earlier, the authors present additional suggestions on how peace journalism should be applied in an African setting.

For example, in Chapter 6, Victor Bwire writes,

> Professional requirements set by the Media Council of Kenya dictate that journalists must look at conflict holistically with the aim of objective, accurate, and reliable reporting. When journalists are equipped with such a wide understanding and approach they are likely to "avoid repeating shallow, thoughtless rhetoric about the conflict to achieve sensationalism and targets for their media houses." Journalism that is conflict-sensitive equips media practitioners with the capacity to recognize that their role is to serve audiences and not to serve as a megaphone for any actor in a propaganda war . . . [We must] build journalists' awareness about the potentially pivotal role they can play in mediating or exacerbating conflict. Such initiatives entail working with the media to find a means of reporting that balances between two disparate positions and emphasizes peace promotion.
>
> (p. 73)

In Chapters 3 and 4, Ogenga introduces Hybrid Peace Journalism (HPJ), a concept that addresses the adaptation of Western peace journalism thought for use in an African context. He writes about PJ's utility in emphasizing truth-telling about conflicting parties in a fair, objective manner "with the overall aim of resolving the conflict by balancing the perspectives of all the parties involved. However, due to contextual factors, peace journalism should be applied in Africa in a manner that responds to local dynamics" (p. 39). The latter is what he expounds by emphasizing the need for community media approaches to peacebuilding found in community radio interlinked with social media platforms.

Elaborating specifically on applying HPJ when reporting about terrorism in the region, Ogenga writes,

> HPJ urges journalists to deliberately mention the word *peace* when reporting on terrorism and to avoid stereotyping and inflammatory labels such as "Islamic terrorist," "Muslim terrorist," "Islamic jihadist," and "Somali terrorist" in their news coverage. However, the media uses such words partly because the local educational institutions that train journalists rely on mainstream traditional Western conceptualizations of news and news values. . . . It is therefore useful for African institutions and scholars to reconceptualize the approach toward the training of journalists and practice of journalism in Africa. Such a new approach should be context-sensitive and rich in African values, particularly those relating to peace, for journalists to integrate African peace-centered perspectives when covering acts of terrorism.
>
> (p. 39)

Such an approach, Jacinta Mwende Maweu writes in Chapter 7, cannot leave behind the basics of good journalism. She observes that

> [j]ournalists should not only report events; they should also provide in-depth analysis to put issues into context. Through in-depth analysis and the bringing together of multiple perspectives, journalists create the potential for a more knowledgeable, well-rounded, and aware public. This increased awareness could lead to a stronger civil society and a more active population that can stand up for its civil, political, and socioeconomic rights, which are grossly violated during times of conflict. Good journalism grounded on a peace and human rights framework should not avoid the ugly facts. It should instead accurately report on what is going on, interrogate the claims, and report them in a manner that helps

the reader, listener, or viewer understand what is happening. Such reporting would also help in holding perpetrators to account.

(p. 79)

Before PJ can be applied or implemented in Africa, the authors note that a number of obstacles, some of them unique to East Africa, must be overcome.

In Chapter 2, Gloria Laker discusses the difficulty of balancing stories, a key PJ tenet, during wartime. She writes that during the Lord's Resistance Army war in Uganda, "We had no access to the rebels, which meant that we frequently gave one-sided reports" (p. 16). Also, providing accurate reporting, another PJ emphasis, was difficult because of propaganda. Laker writes, "The few LRA collaborators we knew gave us contradictory and diversionary information, so we could not trust them" (p. 16).

Western influence also impedes peace journalism. Ogenga argues that Kenyan journalists, and other African journalists, are challenged to adapt HPJ because they are heavily influenced by "Western values and paradigms." He writes,

> Arguably, the Western media has been responsible for setting the pattern for how global media frames and covers terrorism. Domestic politics in Western countries had an outsized impact on the discourse around what constitutes terrorism and who is a terrorist . . .
>
> (p. 41)

Because of this, Ogenga notes,

> Francis B. Nyamnjoh argues that the assumptions underpinning African journalistic practices are not informed by the fact that Africans should be involved in Africanizing their modernity and modernizing their Africanity. Therefore, a complex narrative that goes far beyond the simplistic Western one regarding Africa is necessary.
>
> (p. 43)

Inter- and intra-ethnic group conflicts also present challenges to peace journalists throughout East Africa. In Chapter 5, John Oluoch discusses one conflict involving the Abakuria community. Like many other instances of intra-ethnic conflict in Kenya, Oluoch writes, this one is based on

> clan differences and has led to extensive destruction and death without regard to gender and age. The construction of clan identity

in the Abakuria ethnic community has increasingly been used as the basis for the allocation of political offices. Scholars have argued that the Abakuria conflict has become perpetual.

(p. 56)

Another challenge, according to Oluoch, is that

the real scale and magnitude of the Abakuria conflict do not get prominent coverage in the mainstream national [Kenyan] media. What is normally reported is cattle theft among the Abakuria, with hardly any indication about the magnitude or impact of the so-called cattle theft. It is therefore not clear how the mass media has assisted in the resolution of the intra-ethnic conflicts in Abakuria.

(p. 61)

East African journalists also face legal obstacles as they seek to improve their reporting. Bwire writes,

Media support groups in Kenya are aware of the limitations jour-nalists face. Several measures were put in place ahead of the 2017 general election to strengthen existing laws regulating media cov-erage of political and ethnic violence and terrorism. These include the Prevention of Terrorism Act and the National Intelligence Ser-vice Act in 2012, the Proceeds of Crime and Anti-Money Laun-dering Act in 2009, and the Prevention of Organized Crime Act in 2010. In addition, a number of administrative pronouncements and policy statements have been made by the authorities targeted at the media, clearly indicating that the media must change the way it covers matters of national security.

(p. 67)

There are obstacles to journalists specific to covering terrorism in the region, according to several authors. Bwire observes, "A major chal-lenge facing journalists covering terrorism and security-related events is increased conflict with Kenya's security institutions. Journalists have experienced intimidation, physical attacks, trauma, loss of equipment, and some have also been co-opted by the government" (p. 68).

The influence of elites can also impede PJ. Jacinta Mwende Maweu, in Chapter 7, argues that

the major impediment to a peace and human rights approach to journalism lies in the media's structural subordination to the interests of political and economic elites. . . . Although members of the media are not simply agents of the powerful, there is a vast body of scholarly literature that suggests that news media focuses on powerful people and institutions and generally reflects established interests. The way the media uses language to represent different social and political groups and to describe what events and issues are newsworthy tends to establish the dominant ways the rest of us to talk about those groups and events.

(p. 75)

The authors, undaunted by these obstacles, present useful strategies on how these challenges can be overcome.

For example, Ogenga writes that peace journalism can be adapted into hybrid peace journalism through the use of "Campus Community Radio for Peacebuilding" managed by students or "Campus Peace Ambassadors." He writes,

These community radio stations will play two roles: first, they will act as training facilities for upcoming journalists. Second, they will be used as peacebuilding spaces for addressing peace and security issues such as conflict, youth radicalization, and violent extremism. This will enable young people to exit violence, learn to explore various types of peacebuilding, and nurture resilient communities through action learning. This underscores the salience of institutional training in universities on news reporting and peace-centered news coverage in Africa.

(p. 45)

Oluoch agrees that community-based, local-language media can be a powerful tool. He writes that these media outlets "provide a set of participatory communication techniques that support community dialogue by using local languages to communicate directly with community members, including youth and women, regarding issues of importance to that specific community" (p. 59).

Oluoch emphasizes the utility of local language broadcasting. He writes,

Local broadcasting is instrumental in helping developing countries like Kenya combat economic, political, educational, health, and social-cultural challenges. Ethnic tensions, human rights abuses, and corruption in government can be addressed through vernacular radio programs. Low literacy levels in rural areas and health issues, such as infant mortality, maternal deaths, and communicable diseases, are best addressed through tailor-made radio programs broadcast in various vernacular languages through the radio – since radio is cheap and accessible through ordinary internet-enabled cell phones.

(p. 58)

Armed with these good ideas, and a desire to improve journalism in East Africa, PJ enthusiasts have sponsored numerous peace journalism projects and initiatives in the region. Oluoch writes,

Most [projects] focus on professional training initiatives to promote better coverage of issues related to diverse identities or differences and encourage reports on peace initiatives. The Canadian-based Institute for Media Policy and Civil Society suggests five kinds of peace interventions, including training, promoting positive images, and providing fictional storylines that have a positive peace message. Some of these approaches are little more than applying the best techniques of professional journalism to conflict reporting.

(p. 65)

Hundreds of journalists have been trained in peace journalism techniques throughout Uganda by the Center for Global Peace Journalism, Internews, and others. In addition, Laker writes, "A number of non-governmental organizations have partnered with peace journalists in the region to produce messages about peaceful reconciliation, many of which still play on some radio stations today" (p. 18).

Indeed, the practice of PJ in Uganda during the time of the 2011 election was encouraged by a peace and electoral journalism project featuring 50 or so seminars sponsored by USAID, the Uganda Media Development Foundation, and the Center for Global Peace Journalism. The result of the project, confirmed through an extensive study, was that there was no media-induced election violence and that, further, the lack of violence was attributable to the PJ project in 2010–11. In both Kenya and Uganda, the more responsible PJ techniques journalists used to cover elections in 2013 and 2011 stand in stark contrast to previous election coverage that helped to stoke sectarianism and, in the case of Kenya in 2008, inflamed violence between ethnic groups that took 800 lives.

Peace journalism is now visible in both professional and academic settings. Laker discusses Radio Freedom, a community-based peace radio exemplar of peace journalism that was "geared toward conflict resolution by promoting the peace process" (p. 17). Today, Radio Freedom is called Mega FM, and it continues to broadcast messages of peace and reconciliation from its base in Gulu in northern Uganda.

Meanwhile, HPJ is being implemented at the Center for Media, Democracy, Peace, and Security at Rongo University in Kenya, which launched a new graduate program in Media, Democracy, Peace, and Security and a Visiting Post-Doctoral Fellowship Program based on peace journalism. In addition, "CMDPS has institutionalized a new philosophical approach to peace journalism research in Africa by developing hybrid peace journalism," Ogenga writes (p. 48).

Peace journalism projects and programs have also been held in Rwanda and South Sudan, where seminars for journalists were held in 2016 under the auspices of the Association of Media Development in South Sudan.

Given peace journalism's applicability and growing acceptance in East Africa, it's clear that PJ's future in the region is a bright one. As this book goes to press, large-scale PJ training and implementation projects, potentially financed by governments, academic institutions, and NGOs, are being planned for both Kenya and Uganda. In addition, the exponential growth of online and social media in the region will offer nearly unlimited opportunities to disseminate PJ-style news and information.

My textbook *Peace Journalism Principles and Practices* concludes with optimism that

> journalism can get better, and can adopt at least some of the principles of peace journalism, despite the obstacles. . . . While the goal of news media practicing peace journalism is admirable, perhaps a more realistic goal would be the integration of peace journalism into the journalism curricula at universities in the U.S. and worldwide. Peace journalism, like the time-honored journalistic tradition of objectivity, is an ideal. Any progress toward this ideal, towards better, more responsible reporting, will make the journey worthwhile.

With palpable enthusiasm among journalists and academics in East Africa for PJ, one can easily foresee a vibrant and dynamic future for proponents of more responsible peace reporting.

Appendices

Appendix I

List of workshop participants and their email addresses

1 Mercy Tyra Murengu
   Kenyamurengumercie@gmail.com

2 Joseph Oduha, Southern Sudan
   Abunabet@gmail.com

3 Willy Chowoo, Uganda
   Choowilly@gmail.com

4 Margaret Matunda, Kenya
   Merymaggy@gmail.com

5 Sila Koskei, Kenya
   Silahk70@gmail.com

6 Godfrey Lutego, Tanzania
   Gratianagodfrey@gmail.com

7 Twagira Wilson, Rwanda
   Twagiwils@gmail.com

8 Kassim Muhammed Adinasi
   Kassimadinasi84@gmail.com

9 Abalo Irene, Uganda
   Irene.abalo@gmail.com

10 Wycliffe Masinde, Kenya
   Wycmasinde@gmail.com

11 Lilian Ndege, Kenya
    Lilndege@yahoo.com

12 Giramahoro Richard, Rwanda (did not make it)
    Girichard2000@yahoo.fr

Appendix II

List of workshop facilitators

Steven Youngblood is an associate professor and the director of the Center for Global Peace Journalism, Park University, USA. He is also the editor in chief of the *Peace Journalist Magazine*.

Gloria Laker is the director of the Peace Journalism Foundation East Africa in Uganda and a former war and peace reporter on the northern Uganda Lord Resistant Army conflict.

Fredrick Ogenga is an Associate Professor of Communication and Media Studies, Head of the Department of Communication Journalism and Media Studies, Rongo University, Founding Director of the Center for Media, Democracy, Peace and Security, Rongo University and Chief Executive Officer, The Peacemaker Corps Foundation, Kenya.

John Oluoch is a Senior Lecturer Department of Communication, Journalism and Media Studies, Rongo University and Director of the Rongo University's Privately Sponsored Students Directorate.

Victor Bwire is the deputy chief executive officer of the Media Council of Kenya.

Jacinta Mwende is a Senior Lecturer in the Department of Philosophy and Adjunct lecturer in the School of Journalism and Media Studies The University of Nairobi.

Appendix III

Call for proposals

CALL FOR PROPOSALS: REGIONAL PEACE JOURNALISM TRAINING WORKSHOP
African Peacebuilding Network (APN) SSRC and Center for Media, Democracy Peace and Security, Rongo University

The African Peacebuilding Network (APN) of the Social Science Research Council (SSRC) in partnership with the Center for Media, Democracy, Peace and Security (CMDPS), Rongo University is organizing a two day Regional Peace Journalism Workshop for Eastern Africa to be held at the Center for Media, Democracy, Peace and Security (Rongo University, Kenya). The workshop will expose between 12–15 (equally distributed between women and men) media practitioners: journalists and editors from Kenya, Uganda, Tanzania, Rwanda, Ethiopia, and Burundi (radio, TV, newspaper and online) to the key concepts and issues in peace journalism, including reflections on the role of the media in conflict mediation and peacebuilding in East African countries.

Content

The workshop will include topics such as essentials of Hybrid Peace Journalism, conflict, justice, and reconciliation. Part of the training will promote better understanding of three African philosophies of *Umoja* or unity, *Harambee* or together and *Utu* or humanity "you are because we are" in relation to peace journalism. It will also sensitize them to best practices in the adoption of a peace journalism approach as well as the ethics of reporting about sensitive issues, including acts of terrorism. Proposal of about 500 words should be sent to the project coordinator Dr. Fredrick Ogenga: ogengafredrick@gmail.com copied to apn@ssrc.org before 25 of February 2015. The workshop organizers will meet all the costs related to the workshop for successful applicants which will include return air tickets, accommodation and meals for the entire duration of the workshop. Participants are expected to come to the workshop with samples of their work/reports, which will be discussed in a practical training session.

Dates: from 16th March to 17th March, 2017

Expected output(s)

Participants are expected to have a better understanding of the concept and practice of peace journalism, including how to apply such knowledge in reporting violent conflict. It is also expected that they will be informed about the activities of the APN and contribute to the building of the network, particularly in relation to building connections between media practitioners and scholars in Eastern Africa. The final output from the workshop will be an edited e-book titled **"African Peace Journalism – A Guide for Scholars and Practitioners"** consisting of six chapters. Contributions will be expected from each of the instructors which include one practitioner.

Appendix IV

Workshop program

RONGO UNIVERSITY'S CENTERFOR MEDIA, DEMOCRACY, PEACE AND SECURITY-SOCIAL SCIENCE RESEARCH COUNCIL'S AFRICA PEACEBUILDING NETWORK REGIONAL AFRICA PEACE JOURNALISM TRAINING WORKSHOP, GREAT LAKES HOTEL, KISUMU, KENYA
Final programme
16th–17th March 2017

Thursday, 16th March 2017

8:00–8:45	Registration
8:45–9:00	Opening Remarks (Session Chair, Dr. Fredrick Ogenga – Center for Media, Democracy, Peace and Security, Rongo University, Kenya)
9:00–10:30	Prof. Steven Youngblood (Peace Journalism in a Global Perspective-Center for Global Peace Journalism, Park University, USA)
10:30–11:00	**Tea Break & Group Photo**
11:00–12:30	Dr. Jacinta Mwende (Peace Journalism and Human Rights-Nairobi University, Kenya)
12:30–2:00	**Lunch Break** (Session Chair, Dr. Jacinta Mwende)
2:00–3:30	Dr. Fredrick Ogenga (Thinking about Community Radio and Beyond for Conflict Management in The North Rift: A Concept Paper)
3:30–4:00	**Coffee Break**
4:00–4:45	Dr. Fredrick Ogenga (First Day Session Wrap Up)

Friday, 17th March 2017

8:00–8:45	Registration
8:45–9:00	Opening Remarks (Session Chair, Dr. Duncan Omanga)
9:00–10:30	Dr. Fredrick Ogenga (Hybrid Peace Journalism: Institutional Philosophical Approaches to Peace and Security in Africa)
10:30–11:00	**Tea Break**
11:00–12:00	Gloria Laker (Peace Journalism in the LRA conflict, Former War and Peace Reporter on Northern Uganda LRA Conflict, Peace Journalism Foundation East Africa, Uganda Kenya)
12:00–13:00	John Oluoch, Repositioning Social Responsibility Theory in Defense of Vernacular Mass Media in Kenya. Rongo University
13:00–2:00	**Lunch Break** (Session Chair, Dr Fredrick Ogenga)
2:00–3:30	Victor Bwire (Media, Elections and Peace: Do Journalists need Different Skills? Media Council of Kenya)
3:30–4:00	**Coffee Break**
4:00–4:45	Steven Youngblood (Second day session Wrap Up)
5:00	Closing (Dr Fredrick Ogenga)

Index

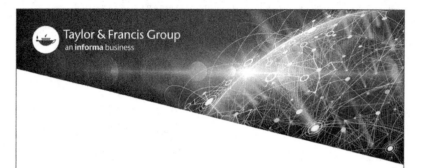

Printed in the United States
by Baker & Taylor Publisher Services